THE BOY INVENTORS' RADIO-TELEPHONE

RICHARD BONNER

The Boy Inventors' Radio Telephone

Richard Bonner

© 1st World Library, 2006
PO Box 2211
Fairfield, IA 52556
www.1stworldlibrary.com
First Edition

LCCN: 2006936240

Softcover ISBN: 978-1-4218-3104-6
Hardcover ISBN: 978-1-4218-3004-9
eBook ISBN: 978-1-4218-3204-3

Purchase *"The Boy Inventors' Radio Telephone"*
as a traditional bound book at:
www.1stWorldLibrary.com/purchase.asp?ISBN=978-1-4218-3104-6

1st World Library is a literary, educational organization dedicated to:

- Creating a free internet library of downloadable ebooks

- Hosting writing competitions and offering book publishing scholarships.

Interested in more 1st World Library books?
contact: literacy@1stworldlibrary.com
Check us out at: www.1stworldlibrary.com

1st World Library Literary Society

Giving Back to the World

"If you want to work on the core problem, it's early school literacy."

— **James Barksdale, former CEO of Netscape**

"No skill is more crucial to the future of a child, or to a democratic and prosperous society, than literacy."

— **Los Angeles Times**

Literacy... means far more than learning how to read and write... The aim is to transmit... knowledge and promote social participation."

— **UNESCO**

"Literacy is not a luxury, it is a right and a responsibility. If our world is to meet the challenges of the twenty-first century we must harness the energy and creativity of all our citizens."

— **President Bill Clinton**

"Parents should be encouraged to read to their children, and teachers should be equipped with all available techniques for teaching literacy, so the varying needs and capacities of individual kids can be taken into account."

— **Hugh Mackay**

CONTENTS

I. THE POWER OF THE AIR 9
II. AN ENCOUNTER WITH A CHARACTER 14
III. THE PROFESSOR'S DILEMMA 20
IV. "WHERE IS HE?" 26
V. CHESTER CHADWICK--INVENTOR 34
VI. THE RADIO TELEPHONE 40
VII. THE GREAT TEST 46
VIII. TALKING THROUGH SPACE 52
IX. THE BOYS FACE TROUBLE 56
X. AN INVOLUNTARY AERONAUT 61
XI. BY THE ROADSIDE 65
XII. MAKING ENEMIES 70
XIII. THE LEADEN TUBE 76
XIV. IN THE HOSPITAL 81
XV. A TALE OF THE COLORADO 85
XVI. ZEB CUMMINGS 89
XVII. IN THE LABORATORY 93
XVIII. INTO THE STORM 98
XIX. THE "LIGHTNING CAGE" 102
XX. THROUGH THE AIR 106
XXI. VAULTING TO THE RESCUE 110
XXII. "Z. 2. X." 116
XXIII. ON THE BORDER LINE 123
XXIV. "THE THREE BUTTES" 130

XXV. INTO THE BEYOND	134
XXVI. THE START FOR THE UNKNOWN	140
XXVII. THE PROFESSOR'S SECOND DILEMMA	145
XXVIII. THE UPPER REGIONS	150
XXIX. A MUD BATH	155
XXX. NIGHT ON THE COLORADO	159
XXXI. THE ISLAND OF MYSTERY	164
XXXII. THROUGH THE WOODS	168
XXXIII. THE SECRET AT LAST	173
XXXIV. THE INTERLOPERS	178
XXXV. TRIUMPH	184
XXXVI. THE HOMECOMING	190

CHAPTER I

THE POWER OF THE AIR

"That's it, Jack. Let her out!"

"Suffering speed laws of Squantum, but she can travel!" exclaimed Dick Donovan, redheaded and voluble.

"I tell you, electricity is the thing. Beats gasoline a million ways," chimed in Tom Jesson. Tom sat beside his cousin, Jack Chadwick, on the driver's seat of a curious-looking automobile which was whizzing down the smooth, broad, green-bordered road that led to Nestorville, the small town outside Boston where the Boy Inventors made their home.

The car that Jack Chadwick was driving differed in a dozen respects from an ordinary automobile. There was no engine hood in front. Instead of a bonnet the car, which was low slung, long and painted black, had a sharp prow of triangular shape. Its body, in fact, might be roughly compared to the form of a double-ended whaleboat.

As it sped along outside the city limits, and immune from hampering speed laws, the car emitted no sound.

It moved silently, without the usual sharp staccato rattle of the exhaust. Behind it there was no evil-smelling trail of gasoline and oil smoke. The car glided as silently as a summer breeze on its wire-wheels, like those of a bicycle enlarged.

"I'll get a great story out of this," declared Dick Donovan, who, as readers of other volumes of this series know, was a reporter on a Boston paper. "That is, if you'll let me write it," he added, leaning forward over the front seat from the tonneau as he spoke.

"How about it, Jack?" asked Tom with an amused smile. "Shall we let Dick here get famous at our expense again?"

"I don't see why not," said Jack. "Everything about the Electric Monarch is patented. The new reciprocating device, and the self-feeding storage batteries are fully covered. If Dick wants to write a romance about it he can, provided he leaves our pictures out."

"Oh, I'll do that," Dick readily promised. "Are you making top speed now, Jack?"

"Nowhere near; I wouldn't dare to. I believe that the Monarch is capable of ninety miles an hour. I wish we had a place like Ormond Beach to try her out on."

"You can count me out on that," chuckled Dick. "This is fast enough for me."

The boys were trying out their latest invention, an electric car capable of making the speed of a gasoline-driven vehicle, and one which could be operated at a minimum of cost, almost a nominal expense, as compared with the high price of a vehicle run by an explosive engine.

It was the trial trip of the Electric Monarch, as they had decided to call it, and so far the performances of the machine had exceeded, instead of fallen below, their expectations. Dick, who had been invited to the "tryout," was full of questions as they sped silently, and with an absolute lack of vibration, along the road.

"How do you generate your electricity?" he asked eagerly.

"By a device geared to the rear axle," answered Tom. "It runs a sort of dynamo, though it would be difficult for you to understand it if I went into details. It's something like the ordinary generator and turns a constant stream of 'juice' into the storage batteries that, in turn, feed the engines."

"Yes, that's all plain enough," said the inquisitive Dick, "but how do you get your power for starting?"

"If there is not enough juice in the storage batteries for the purpose we resort to compressed air," was the reply from Tom, for Jack, with keen eyes on the unrolling ribbon of road, was too busy to have his attention distracted.

"And that?" Dick paused interrogatively.

"Is pumped into a pressure tank as we go along. See that gauge?" he pointed to one on the dashboard of the car in front of the driver's seat.

Dick nodded.

"Well, that's a pressure gauge. You see, we have sixty pounds of air in the tank now. That can generate enough electricity to start the car going. After that the process is automatic."

"Yes, you explained that. Suppose the tank should, through an accident, be empty, and you wanted to start?"

"We've provided for that"

"I expected so. Wabbling wheels of Wisconsin, you fellows are certainly wonders."

"Nothing very wonderful about it," disclaimed Tom. "Well, if we find the tank is empty we have a powerful, double-acting hand pump by which, without much effort, we can get up any pressure we need."

"And then you turn a valve?"

"Exactly, and the air-motor turns over the dynamo which starts generating electricity right away."

"Then, except for the first cost of the car, the expense of operating it is comparatively nothing?" asked Dick.

"Yes, you might say we get our power out of the air, and that's free—so far."

"And there's no limit, then, to what you can do or where you can go with the Electric Monarch?"

"None; that is, so long as the machinery holds out. We are independent of fuel and the lubricating system is so devised that the oiling is automatic and requires attending to only once a month. We could easily carry a year's supply of lubricant."

"Tall timbers of Taunton!" burst out Dick enthusiastically. "You've solved the problem of the poor man's car. All the owner of an Electric Monarch has to do is to pump a little pump-handle or press a little button and he's off without it costing him a cent. My story will sure make a big sensation!"

"Well, you want to tone down that part about its not costing a cent," chimed in Jack as they coasted down a hill. "The expense of the motor and the self-lubricating bearings and so on is pretty steep. But we hope in time to be able to cheapen the whole car."

They were shooting swiftly down the hill as he spoke. The next moment he looked ahead again as they shot round a curve. As they did so his hand sought a button and an ear-splitting screech arose from a powerful siren.

In the center of the road, quite oblivious to the oncoming automobile, was an odd figure, that of a small man in a rusty, baggy suit of black.

He had a hammer in his hand and was hitting some object in the roadway over which he was bending with a concentrated interest that made him quite unconscious of the onrushing car.

"Hi! Get out of the way!" yelled the boys.

But the man did not look up. Instead, he kept tapping away with his hammer at whatever it was that absorbed his attention so intently.

CHAPTER II

AN ENCOUNTER WITH A "CHARACTER"

Jack jammed down the emergency brakes, which were pneumatic and operated from the pressure tank, with a suddenness that sent Dick Donovan almost catapulting out of the tonneau.

"Jumping jiggers of Joppa!" he shouted, for he had not yet seen the obstacle in the road, "what's happened? Are we bust up?"

"No, but if I hadn't stopped when I did we'd have bust someone else up," declared Jack. "Look there!"

"Can you beat it?" exclaimed Tom.

As the brakes brought the car to a stop within a foot of his stout, rotund figure, the little man in the center of the road looked up with a sort of mild surprise through a pair of astonishingly thick-lensed eyeglasses secured to his ears by a thick, black ribbon. He wore a broad-brimmed black hat and wrinkled, baggy clothes of bar-cloth, and a huge pair of square-toed boots that looked as if their tips had been chopped off with an ax.

Over his shoulder was slung a canvas bag which appeared to be heavy and bulged as if several irregularly shaped, solid substances were inside of it. The spot where this odd encounter took place was some distance from any town, but a bicycle leaning against a tree at the roadside showed how the little man had got there.

"Say, would you mind letting us get by?" asked Jack.

The little man raised a hand protestingly.

"I'll be delighted to in just a moment," he said, "but just now it's impossible. You see, I've just discovered a vein of what I believe to be Laurentian granite running across the road. I am trying to trace it and—what's that? Good gracious! Back up your machine, please. I believe it runs under your wheel. I must make sure."

Jack obligingly threw in the reverse to humor the little man, who darted forward and began scraping up the dust in the road with his hands as if he had been a dog scratching out a rabbit hole. He began chipping away eagerly with his hammer at some rock that cropped up out of the road.

He broke off a piece with his hammer, which was an oddly shaped tool, and drawing out a big magnifying glass scanned the chip intently. He appeared to have forgotten all about the waiting boys. But now he seemed to remember them. He looked up, beaming.

"A magnificent specimen. One of the finest I have ever seen. Most remarkable!"

And with that he popped the bit of stone into his bag, which the boys now saw was filled with similar objects.

"Maybe he'll let us get by now," remarked Tom, but a sudden exclamation from Dick Donovan cut him short.

"Why, hullo, professor," he said, "out collecting specimens?"

The little man peered at him sharply. And then broke into a smile of recognition.

"Why, it's Dick Donovan!" he beamed, hastening up to the car, "the young journalist who wrote an article about my specimens once and woefully mixed them up. However, to an unscientific mind—"

"They are all just rocks," finished Dick with a grin.

"I have had unusual success to-day," said the professor, who appeared not to have heard the remark. "I must have at least fifty pounds of specimens on my back at this minute."

He broke off suddenly. The next moment he darted off to the side of the road and chipped off a fragment of rock from a bank that overhung it.

"This is lucky, indeed," he exclaimed, holding it up to the light so that some specks in the gray stone sparkled. "An extremely rare specimen of mica that I had no idea existed in this part of New England."

The odd little man opened his bag and introduced his latest acquisition into it While he was doing this Dick had been explaining to the boys:

"He's a queer character. Professor Jerushah Jenks. They say he's a great authority on mineralogy and so on. I interviewed him once. He's always out collecting."

"Does he always carry a quarry like that around on his back?" asked Tom.

"Always when he's getting specimens," Dick whispered back.

By this time the professor, his eyes agleam over his latest discovery, was back at the side of the car.

"Ah, my beauty, I have you safe now," he said, patting the side of the bagful of specimens. "Boys, this is my lucky day."

The boys could hardly keep from smiling at the little man's delight. It appeared hard to believe that anyone could find pleasure in packing about a sackful of heavy rocks on a hot day. But the professor's eyes were sparkling. It was clear he considered himself one of the most fortunate of men.

Dick introduced the boys and, to their surprise, the professor declared that he had read of their various adventures and inventions.

"We are actually fellow adventurers in the field of science," he cried, rattling his bag of specimens enthusiastically. "Some time I should like to call on you and see your workshops."

"You will be welcome at any time," said Jack cordially, and then the professor declared that he must be getting home.

"If we are going your way we can give you a ride," said Tom.

"Thank you, I'll accept that invitation. But what an odd-looking automobile you have there."

The boys explained to him that it was a new type of car that they were trying out for the first time and then Dick helped the scientist lift his bicycle into the tonneau. He would have helped him with his weighty load of specimens, but the professor refused to be parted from them. As they started off again he sat with the bag firmly gripped between his knees, as if afraid someone would separate him from it.

The professor lived with a spinster sister to whom his specimens were the bane of her life. As the car rolled swiftly along, he occupied his time by peeping into the bag at frequent intervals to see that none of the specimens, by some freak of nature, flew out.

All at once he reached forward and clutched Jack by the shoulder.

"Stop! My dear young friend, please stop at once!"

"What's the matter?" asked Jack, slowing down at the urgent summons.

"Look! Look there at that rock!"

To Jack the rock in question was just an ordinary bit of stone in a wall fencing in a pasture in which some cattle were grazing. But evidently the professor thought otherwise.

"It's a fine specimen of green granite," he exclaimed. "I must have it. How did such a fine piece ever come to be placed in a common wall?"

The car having now been brought to a stop, he leaped nimbly out, clutching his geological hammer in one hand and his precious sack of specimens in the other. He rushed up to the wall and stood for a minute with his head on one side, like an inquisitive bird.

"Too bad. That stone's a large flat one and goes right through the center of the wall," he mused. "The wall must come down."

And then, to the boys' consternation, he began demolishing the wall, pulling down the stones and throwing them right and left.

"Professor, you'll get in trouble," warned Dick in alarm. "Those cattle will get out. The farmer will be after us."

But the professor paid not the slightest attention. Taking off his coat, he resumed his operations with even greater vigor than before. The cattle in the field eyed him curiously. Then they began to move toward him. In front of the rest of the herd was a big black-and-white animal with sharp horns and big, thick neck.

It gave a sudden bellow and then rushed straight at the considerable gap the man of science had made in the stone fence.

"It's a bull!" yelled Dick suddenly. "Run, professor! Run or he'll toss you!"

With lowered horns the bull rushed down upon the unconscious scientist at locomotive speed. But the professor was oblivious to everything else but uncovering the odd-looking green stone embedded in the heart of the wall.

The boys shouted to him but he didn't hear them. On rushed the bull, bellowing, charging, ready to annihilate the scientist.

"Run!" yelled the boys at the top of their lungs. "Run!"

But the professor, with his precious bag in one hand and his hammer in the other, stood staring at the advancing bull through his thick glasses as if the maddened creature had been some sort of new and interesting specimen.

"Gracious! He's a goner!" groaned Dick.

CHAPTER III

THE PROFESSOR'S DILEMMA

But the professor was seen to suddenly dart, with an activity they would hardly have expected in him, across the road. He was only in the nick of time.

Almost opposite to the gap in the fence he had made was a tree with low-hanging boughs. As the bull charged through the gap, right on his heels, the professor, still with his bag, slung by its leather strap across his shoulders, swung himself up into the lower limbs.

The boys set up a cheer.

"Good for you, professor!" cried Dick, as the bull, with lowered head and horns, charged into the tree and made it shake as if a storm had struck.

"Wow! That's the time he got a headache!" cried Tom excitedly, as the professor, clinging desperately to his refuge, was almost flung from it by the shock.

"Gracious, boys, what shall I do?" he asked, looking about him from his leafy perch with a glance of despair that would have been comical had the situation not been serious, for the bull, instead of accepting his defeat, stood under the tree pawing and ramping ferociously.

"Well, here's a fine kettle of fish!" exclaimed Jack. "What are we going to do now?"

"Blessed if I know," said Dick helplessly. "By the bucking bulls of Bedlam, this is a nice mess."

"Maybe we could throw rocks at him and chase him away," suggested Tom.

"No chance; he's got his eye on the professor," returned Jack, "and if we did get out he would chase us and that wouldn't do the professor any good."

"Can't you help me, boys," inquired the professor in an agonized tone. "This tree limb is not exactly—er—comfortable."

"You're in no danger of falling, are you?" called Jack, in an alarmed voice.

"No—er—that is, I don't think so. But this is an extraordinary position. Most—er—undignified. I'm glad my sister can't see me."

"Try throwing some of the rocks out of your satchel at him," suggested Dick.

But the professor waxed indignant at this proposal.

"And cast my pearls before swine! or rather my specimens before a bull!" exclaimed the professor, in helpless indignation. "No, young gentlemen, not a pebble from this bag is wasted on that creature."

"I'd drop the whole bag on him," said Dick, "if I was in that position. It's heavy enough to knock out an elephant, let alone a bull."

"Can't you suggest anything?" wailed the professor.

"I'm trying to think of something right now," declared Jack, racking his brains for some way out of the predicament.

"I wish the farmer that owned him would come along and get his old bull out of there," said Dick.

"Yes, and then there would be fresh complications," declared Jack.

"How do you make that out?" came from Dick.

"He'll probably know how to handle him," supplemented Tom.

"Yes, he would if he's a bull-fighter," scoffed Dick, "and I never heard of there being any matadors in the vicinity of Nestorville."

"Lots of doormats, though," grinned Tom.

"Say, if you do that again I'll throw you out of the car," cried Jack at this atrocious pun.

"Sorry, couldn't help it. Just slipped out," said Tom contritely.

"Well, you'll slip out if the offense is repeated," retorted Dick. "But," he went on, "seriously, fellows, we've got to do something."

"Try blowing the horn," suggested Tom. "It has scared everything else we met. Horses shy at it, so do other autos. Maybe it will get the bull's goat."

"I'll try it, at all events," said Jack.

He pressed the button and the unearthly screech of the electric auto's siren split the air. But the bull merely cast an inquiring glance in their direction and then resumed his vigil over the professor.

"Boys," wailed the unhappy geologist, "can't you do something, anything? I can't roost in this tree all night, like a bird."

The boys couldn't help grinning at this. With his sharp nose, big spectacles and flapping black garments, the professor did look like a mammoth black crow.

"Reminds me of the fox and the crow," said Dick, in a low voice, to his companions.

"Only, in this case, the fox is a bull, and the piece of cheese is the bag of specimens," added Tom.

They looked about helplessly. There was no farmhouse in sight and the road did not appear to be much traveled.

"We'll have to go for help," declared Jack.

"The only thing to do," agreed Tom.

The professor was hailed. He had climbed to another limb with infinite difficulty, because of the encumbering bag of rocks on his back. He declared that he could manage to get along till the boys came back.

"By a merciful provision of providence," he said whimsically, "bulls can't climb trees. The situation might be worse if it was a bear."

"It would be unbearable," declared Dick to Tom.

"But just the same there's trouble a brewin'," retorted Tom. "I wish that farmer would show up."

"As I said before—I don't," responded Jack, as he prepared to start off.

"Why?"

For answer Jack waved an eloquent hand toward the gap in the stone fence.

"I guess he wouldn't be best pleased to find that his fence had been torn down," explained Jack, as the car drove off, leaving the professor marooned in his tree with the sentinel bull waiting patiently below.

Some distance down the road the boys came to a farmhouse. Several men were working in the field under the direction of a stout, red-faced man. Jack shouted to them, and when the red-faced man came up he explained the situation to him. The man was good-natured, or perhaps he rather liked the idea of a ride in such a novel-looking car. Anyhow, he called three of his hands and told them to get pitchforks.

"Never see a bull I couldn't handle," he said as the men, having returned, scrambled into the car.

"Do you know who it belongs to?" asked Jack, as he turned round and headed back to where they left the luckless professor.

"I reckon it's that big Holstein of Josh Crabtree's. He's pretty near as mean as his owner, and that's considerable."

Jack thought of the hole in the wall and hoped they would reach there before farmer Crabtree, and so avoid serious complications.

He drove at top speed, while the friendly farmer and his workmen clung to the sides of the car and looked rather scared at the rate they were going.

"There's the tree," exclaimed Jack, as they came in sight of it, "and there's the gap in the fence."

"And where's the bull?" asked Tom.

"And where's the professor?" added Dick.

Not a trace of the man of science or of the ferocious animal was to be seen.

"Are you sure you boys didn't dream all this?" asked the red-faced farmer suspiciously.

"There ain't even a cow in sight in the pasture lot," said one of the men.

"I reckon this is some sort of a fool joke," added another.

"It isn't. Indeed, it isn't," protested Jack.

"The professor is some place around," said Tom.

But a lengthy search of the vicinity failed to show anything except that the professor had vanished as if the earth had swallowed him.

CHAPTER IV

"WHERE IS HE?"

"Professor!" hailed Dick, at the top of his lungs.

"Professor!" bawled the farm hands.

The red-faced farmer himself regarded the boys quizzically.

"What sort of a chap is this professor of yours?" he asked with an odd intonation.

"He's a geologist," replied Dick. "Why?"

"Oh, I thought he might be a conjurer," was the rejoinder. "He seems to be pretty good at hiding himself."

"Hark!" exclaimed Jack suddenly, standing at pause and listening intently.

"What's up?" demanded Dick, instantly on the alert, too.

"I heard something. It sounded like—"

"There it is again," cried Tom.

A faint, far-off cry, impossible to locate, was borne to their ears.

"It's a call for help," declared Dick.

"That's what it is," agreed the red-faced farmer. "Must be that perfusser of yours, but where in the name of Sam Hill is he?"

It was a puzzling question. The faint cries appeared to be muffled in some way. They looked about them, endeavoring to locate their source. Suddenly one of the farm hands spoke.

"I used to work fer old Crabtree," he said. "There's an old well hereabouts somewheres and maybe he's fell down that."

"Where is it?" demanded Jack.

"Back in the meadow yonder," said the man, pointing in the direction of the pasture lot.

"Let's go over there and see at once," said Dick. "Frantic frogs of France, if the professor's tumbled into a well he may be in serious trouble."

They set off on the run to where a pile of stones showed a well-curb had once been. The hoards at the top, which had covered it over, had rotted, and there was a jagged hole in them. Jack cautiously bent over and placed his mouth at the edge of the hole.

"Professor, are you down there?" he hailed.

"Y-y-y-y-yes," came up in feeble, stuttering tones. "I'm almost frozen. I'm hanging above the water but I can't hold on much longer. The bag of specimens is too heavy."

"Throw it away," urged Jack.

"N-n-n-not for worlds," was the reply. "I was looking for another rare bit of quartz when I fell in here."

"I'll run to the car," said Jack, who had made out that the well was not very deep. "Fortunately, we've got a rope and tackle in there. Hold on, professor, we'll soon have you out."

He hurriedly explained the situation to the others and ran at top speed to the car, in which the boys—like most careful motorists, who never know when such a piece of apparatus may come in useful for hauling a car out of mud or sand, for instance, or for towing an unlucky autoist home—had a block and tackle stowed.

He was soon back, and the rope was lowered to the professor, who made it fast under his arms. Then, aided by the husky muscles of the farm hands, they soon drew him to the surface. But his weight was materially added to by the stones, and it was no light task to rescue him, dripping and shivering, from the dark, cold shaft.

He explained that soon after they had gone some men came up and drove the bull away. But they had seen the gap in the stone wall first.

"They were positively violent," declared the professor, "and said that they'd have the man who did it arrested if they could find him. Under the circumstances, I deemed it prudent to stay up in the tree, where they could not see me. They drove the bull off into another pasture. As soon as the coast was clear I climbed down, but I happened to see a rare bit of quartz sparkling in the sun on the edge of the well-curb. Imprudently I stood on the planking and fell in."

"Gracious, it's a lucky thing you weren't drowned, with all that weight round your neck," declared Jack.

"It was fortunate," said the scientist mildly, as if such a thing as drowning was an everyday occurrence. "As a matter of fact, if I hadn't succeeded in grasping a projecting stone and held on, I might have gone down. It was an—er—a most discomforting experience."

"Well, of all things," exclaimed the red-faced man, "to go trapesing round the country collecting rocks!"

"Not rocks, sir—geological specimens," rejoined the professor with immense dignity, "and—great Huxley! Under your foot, sir! Under your foot!"

"What is it, a snake?" yelled the farmer, jumping backward as the scientist dashed at him with a wild expression.

"No, sir, but a remarkably fine specimen of what appears to be a granolithic substance," exclaimed the professor, and he beganenergetically chipping at a rock upon which the farmer had been standing.

"Crazy as a loon," declared the farmer, winking at his men. "Gets nearly drowned in a well and then begins chopping at a rock as soon as he gets out."

"Oh, this has been a lucky day for me," said the professor with huge satisfaction, as he placed his latest acquisition in the satchel. "As fine a specimen, boys, as ever I encountered," he declared, turning to the boys.

"Gracious," exclaimed Tom and Dick in low tones, "does he call getting chased by a bull and then tumbling down a well a satisfactory day?"

"I should call it a rocky time," grinned Dick.

But at this moment further conversation was cut short by the sudden arrival of a gray-haired, short little old man with a tuft of gray whiskers on his chin.

"Josh Crabtree!" exclaimed the red-faced farmer.

"Wow! now the music starts," declared Dick.

Josh Crabtree, his face ablaze, and his small, malignant eyes sparkling angrily, emitted a roar like that of his Holstein that had caused the professor so much tribulation.

"Say, be you the pesky varmints that tore down my fence and scared my bull out'n two years' growth?" he bellowed.

"I removed some stones from your fence, sir," said the professor, "but it was in the interests of science. You may not have been aware of it, but embedded in your enclosing structure was a fine specimen of green granite."

"Great hopping water-melyuns!" roared Old Crabtree, "and you tore down my fence to git at a pesky bit of rock?"

"Rock to you, sir," responded the scientist calmly, "like the man in the poem a 'primrose by the river's brim, a yellow primrose is to you, and it is nothing more.'"

"Dad rot yer yaller primroses," yelled Old Crabtree, dancing about in his rage. "You make good for tearing down my fence, d'ye hear me?"

"I shall take great pleasure in forwarding you a check for any damage I may have done," said the professor.

"I want ther money now," said the farmer truculently.

"I regret that I have left my wallet at home," said the professor. Then he brightened suddenly. "I can leave my bag of specimens with you as security," he said, "if you will promise to be careful with them."

He unslung his bag and tendered it to the angry farmer who received it with a look of amazement that the next moment turned to wrath when he saw its contents.

"By hickory, what kind of a game is this?" he demanded. "Nothing but a lot of old rocks. By heck, thar's enough here to build a new fence!"

He flung the bag down indignantly just as the professor darted forward with one of his odd, swift movements. He shoved Old Crabtree back without ceremony and bending swiftly to the spot where the angry farmer had been standing he picked up and pocketed a small rock.

"Wa'al land o' Goshen," gasped out the farmer, bewildered. "What in ther name of time is this?"

"A splendid specimen of gneiss," explained the professor triumphantly, "and now, Mr.—er—you were saying?"

"That I wants ter be paid fer ther damage ter my fence."

"How much do you want?" asked Jack, coming to the rescue.

"Reckon a dollar'll be about right."

"If you will let me lend it to you till we reach your home, I'll be very glad to pay him," said Jack aside to the professor.

"But, my dear young friend, there is no necessity. He has ample security till I can send him a check. Why, that bag of specimens is worth fifty dollars at least."

"Them old rocks," sniffed the farmer, who had overheard this last remark, "I wouldn't give yer ten cents fer a cartload uv 'em. They're too small fer fences an' too big to throw at cows."

"You'd better let me pay him," said Jack, and the professor finally consented to this arrangement.

This done, they started back on the run to the professor's home, which was about three miles off. On the way they dropped the red-faced farmer and his hands, who clearly regarded the professor as some sort of an amiable lunatic. But that worthy man, supremely happy despite his wet clothes, was quite contented, and from time to time dipped into his satchel, like a bookworm into a favorite volume, and drew out a particularly valued specimen and admired it.

They soon reached his home, a pretty cottage on the outskirts of Creston, a small town with elm-shaded streets. The professor invited the boys to accompany him into the house. They were met in the passage by a shrill-voiced woman who looked like the professor in petticoats.

"My sister, Miss Melissa," said the professor. "My dear, these are—"

But he got no further in his introduction. Miss Melissa's hands went up in the air and her voice rose in a shrill shriek as she saw her brother's condition.

"Lan's sakes, Jerushah, where have you been?" she exclaimed.

"My dear, I must apologize for my condition," said the professor mildly. "You see I—"

"You're dripping a puddle on my carpets. You're wringing wet through!" shrilled Miss Melissa.

"Yes, you see, my dear, I've been down a well," explained the man of science calmly.

"Do tell! Down a well, Jerushah? At your time of life!"

"You see I was after specimens, my dear," went on the professor.

"Specimens!" exclaimed Miss Melissa. "The whole house is full of old rocks now, Jerushah, an' you have ter go down a well to get more."

"These are very valuable, my dear," said the professor, floundering helplessly.

"Oh, don't tell me. A passel of old rocks. I'm going to get you a hot mustard footbath and some herb tea right away," and without another word, except something about "death of cold, passel of boys," the good lady flounced off.

"She's like that sometimes, but she means well, Melissa does," explained the professor, with a rather sheepish look as he stood in the midst of a puddle that was rapidly converting him into an isolated island in the midst of Miss Melissa's immaculate hall carpet. Suddenly, with one of his impulsive movements, he darted off into a room opening off the hall and came back with a dollar bill he had unearthed from a desk. He handed it to Jack, and then, raising his finger to his lips, he said:

"Don't let Melissa see it. She's the best of women, is Melissa, but peculiar about some things—er—very peculiar."

"Je-ru-shah!" came Miss Melissa's voice.

"Yes, my dear, coming," said the professor, and shouldering his bag of specimens he shook hands with the boys and hastened off to answer his sister's dictatorial call.

"I guess we'd better be going," said Jack, with a smile that he could not repress.

The others agreed, and they were soon speeding back to High Towers, as the estate of Jack's father, also a noted inventor, was called, with plenty to talk about as a result of the events of the day.

CHAPTER V

CHESTER CHADWICK—INVENTOR

As readers of the preceding volumes of this series, know, Jack Chadwick and Tom Jesson, his cousin, had won the titles of Boy Inventors through their ingenuity and mechanical genius. Jack's father, Chester Chadwick, was an inventor of note, and unlike the majority of inventors, he had turned his devices to such good account that he had accumulated a substantial fortune and was able to maintain a fine estate, already referred to as High Towers where, with splendidly equipped workshops and a miniature lake, he could experiment and work out his ideas.

In the first book of this series it was related how Tom Jesson, Jack's cousin, came to make his home at High Towers. Tom's father, an explorer of international fame, had departed on an expedition to Yucatan and had not been heard from since that time. This volume, which was called the Boy Inventors' Wireless Triumph, told of the boys' exploits in the radio-telegraphic field and the uses to which they were able to turn them. In a flying machine, the invention of Mr. Chadwick, they discovered Tom's father, under remarkable circumstances, a prisoner of a tribe of savages, and also found a fortune in precious stones.

In the succeeding story of their adventures, the boys helped an inventor in trouble. The Boy Inventors' Vanishing Gun, as this volume was entitled, set forth in a graphic way the triumph of the boys over the machinations of a gang of rascals intent on stealing the plans of the wonderful implement of warfare which they had helped bring to successful completion.

We next encountered the lads in the Boy Inventors' Diving Torpedo Boat. Here they were placed in a new environment on the surface and in the depths of the ocean. The way in which the wonderful diving craft aided Uncle Sam in a crisis with enemies of the United States was told, and their ingenuity and bravery played no small part in the affair.

The Boy Inventors' Flying Ship was devoted to a detailed narrative of the boys' long and unexpected cruise to the unexplored regions of the Upper Amazon. The boys were shipwrecked and cast away without an apparent hope of rescue on a yacht belonging to a German scientist, the crew of which had mutinied. The boys' capture by a strange tribe and subsequent escape in their Flying Ship formed thrilling portions of this story, while Dick Donovan's researches in natural history provided the boys with a lot of fun.

The volume immediately preceding this showed the boys coming to the rescue of a poor lad, a waif and orphan, who yet had a fortune in the plans and specifications of a new type of craft invented by his dead father who had lacked the capital to develop it. Enemies strove desperately to secure the papers, and even went to the length of forging a will for the purpose, but partly through the agency of an odd German lad, Heiney Pumpernickel Dill, their schemes were frustrated and the invention was developed and set upon a working basis. This book was called the Boy Inventors' Hydroaeroplane, and dealt with some astonishing adventures and perils all of which the boys encountered with plucky spirits and resourceful minds.

For some weeks preceding the opening of the present book relating of the Boy Inventors, Mr. Chadwick had been closeted in his own private laboratory. The boys had seen him only at rare intervals, and then he had appeared abstracted and preoccupied. This, the boys knew, was a sure sign that he was at work on a new idea.

Sometimes the lights burned in his laboratory far into the night and in the morning he would appear at breakfast pale and silent. The boys had indulged in much speculation as to what the new invention could be, but had arrived at no satisfactory conclusion when, two days after their experience with the eccentric professor, Mr. Chadwick summoned them to his private workshop. The boys, who had been at work on the Wondership, the flying automobile with which they had met such surprising adventures in Brazil, obeyed the summons with alacrity. It was delivered to them by Jupe, the negro factotum of the place.

"Massa Chadwick send me on de bustelbolorium," explained Jupe, who had a vocabulary that was all his own, "for yo' alls to come right away by his laburnumtory."

"All right, Jupe, we'll be right over," said Jack, "just as soon as we've got some of this grease off our hands."

The boys' workshop was equipped with a washbasin and they soon made themselves presentable. Then they hurried to Mr. Chadwick's workshop. They found him standing before a roughly-built table on which were ranged some odd-looking bits of apparatus.

There was a gasoline motor in one corner, geared to a generator—or what appeared to be one—from which feed wires led to a square metal box on the table. Attached to this metal box was a sort of horn-shaped mouthpiece something like the transmitter of a telephone. Hanging from its side was what looked like an enlarged telephone receiver. Jack regarded his father questioningly.

"You sent for us, dad?"

"Yes, Jack," was the reply. "I'm in a quandary. Have you any idea what this apparatus is?"

Both boys shook their heads.

"Looks like some kind of a telephone," ventured Tom.

"It is a telephone," replied Mr. Chadwick.

"But—but—where are the wires?" asked Jack, glancing about him, "or haven't you connected it up yet?"

"It's connected up as much as it will ever be," said Mr. Chadwick with a smile. "Can't you guess what it is?"

"I've got it," cried Jack suddenly. "It's a wireless telephone."

"That's right," admitted his father, and, in response to a flood of questions from the boys, he told them how he had been working day and night to bring the device to perfection.

"Now," he said, as he concluded, "I want you boys to go down to that shed that was put up last week at the northwest corner of the orchard."

"The one that was put up to store gasoline?" asked Tom.

"I said it was for that purpose in order to avoid questions till I had my work completed," said Mr. Chadwick with a smile. "Here is the key to it. Inside you will find an apparatus similar to this one. Start the dynamo and then stand in front of the transmitter and place the receiver to your ear. If you don't hear anything at once use the inductor to tune your aerial earth circuit to the transmitted current from my end just exactly as you would tune up a wireless telegraph instrument to catch certain wave lengths from another instrument"

"Then the principle of the radio telephone is the same as that of the wireless telephone?" asked Tom.

"I'll explain that to you later in as plain language as I can," said the inventor, "but now I am anxious to see how this instrument will transmit sound."

The boys were excited. Anything novel in the way of science attracted their bright, active minds as an electromagnet attracts steel. The idea of a wireless telephone, of the possibility of transmitting actual speech through space, just as the dots and dashes of the wireless telegraph are sped through the ether, quickened their inventive faculties to the highest pitch. Both felt a glow of pride that they had been selected, even before their father's scientific friends, to make the first test of this wonderful new invention.

They hurried across the broad lawn that intervened between the workshops and the orchard where the newly erected shed stood, and which, it had been given out, was to serve for the storage of gasoline. Unlocking the door, they found inside an apparatus resembling in almost every detail the one in Mr. Chadwick's workshop.

Jack's hands fairly trembled as he started up the motor and the generator began to buzz. With shining eyes and throbbing pulses he placed the receiver to his ear as his father had directed. But the next moment a flood of disappointment swept through him.

"Well?" demanded Tom, himself a tiptoe with expectation.

"Nothing doing," replied Jack, shaking his head. "I guess the thing isn't at a practical stage yet."

"Wait a minute, give it a chance," urged Tom. "By the way, how about that tuning device, have you tried that yet?"

"No, good gracious, my head must be turning into solid ivory from the neck up. I guess that's just what the trouble is."

Jack began carefully sliding a small block connected to the instruments up and down the coiled wire which formed the tuning apparatus, and brought the sending and receiving ends into harmony just as if they had been two musical instruments. When the right electric "chord" was struck he should be able to hear, just as in wireless he would be able to catch the message of an instrument whose wave lengths were attuned to his.

Suddenly Tom saw his chum and cousin give a start and then a shout. Over the space between the workshop and the small shed a human voice had been borne on electric waves. Sharp and clear as though he had been listening to a "wire" 'phone, Jack caught and recognized his father's voice:

"Hul-lo!"

CHAPTER VI

THE RADIO TELEPHONE

Back and forth through space they talked for quite a time. The boys were jubilant. The despair of many inventors, the wireless or radio telephone appeared to be an accomplished fact. But they didn't dream how much yet remained to be done. At length Mr. Chadwick told them to "hang-up" and come back to the workshop.

The boys were glad to do this for they were extremely anxious to learn something of the forces controlling this aerial method of conversation. So far, they had not the least understanding, beyond a general idea, of how the thing was done. Of the details by which Mr. Chadwick had worked out this radical departure in telephony, they knew nothing.

"Well, what did you think of it, boys?" asked Mr. Chadwick when they returned to the workshop.

"Wonderful, beyond anything I could have imagined," declared Jack.

"How far will it work?" asked Tom.

"That's just the point," said Mr. Chadwick. "That's where I'm at sea. I need a metal of greater conductivity than any attainable to get real results. The carbon that I am using does not throw off enough radio activity to produce a sufficient number of electric impulses to the atmosphere."

Jack and Tom looked puzzled.

"You don't understand me I see," said Mr. Chadwick.

"No, I must say I don't," said Jack; "you see—"

"It's pretty technical," broke in Tom.

"Well, then I'll try to explain to you, in simple language, the general principles of radio telephony," said Mr. Chadwick. "In the first place you know, of course, from your wireless studies, that an electric wave sent into the air will travel till it strikes something, such as an aerial."

"To use the old illustration, an electric impulse sent into the air spreads out in all directions just like the ripples from a stone chucked into a mill-pond," said Jack.

"That's it," said Mr. Chadwick. "Now then, as you also know the wire telephone works by a metal disc in the receiver, vibrating in exactly the same way as does the microphone in the transmitter. According to the vibrations of the voice of the person sending the spoken message, the electric current along the wire, acted upon by the microphone in the transmitter, increases or decreases. This increasing and decreasing current acts on a thin metal disc or diaphragm in the receiver which is held to the ear of the person listening to the message."

"That's plain sailing so far," said Jack. "For instance, when you say 'Hullo' over a phone, the microphone or transmitter gets busy and records it in electrical impulses and shoots it all along the wire where the receiver picks it up and wiggles the metal disc inside it to just the same tune."

"That's it exactly," said Mr. Chadwick. "Now we are ready to go a step further. Now, as this metal disc is attracted or released by the current coming over the wire, it compresses or rarefies the air between it and the ear-drum of the person to whose oral cavity it is held. In this way the sensation of the same sound as was spoken at the transmitter end is reproduced at the receiver end. In other words, the transmitter jerks and jumps just as the needle of a phonograph does in traveling over a record, and transmits these jerks and jumps over the wire to the metal disc which by aerial pressure on the ear drums of the receiver of the message, causes the aural membrane to translate the words, or vibrations along the nerves, to the brain.

"Following up this line," said Mr. Chadwick, "we find that the problem in radio telephony is the same as that met with in ordinary wire telephony. That is to say, we are required to cause a distant metal disc to repeat every inflection of the transmitter. But in the case of radio telephony the result is to be obtained by Hertzian waves, instead of by a current passing through an insulated wire."

"The same sort of waves that are employed in wireless telegraphy?" asked Tom.

"Just the same, only in radio telephony we are confronted by a problem not met with in wireless telegraphy. We have not only to transmit
sound, such as isolated dots and dashes, but to send through the air
every rise and fall and inflection of the human voice just as it is recorded in the minute lines of a phonographic record.

"Experiments have shown that articulation, that is, understand, a speech, depends upon overtones and upper harmonies of a frequency of 5,000 or 8,000 or more."

"What do you mean by frequency?" asked Tom.

"Speaking in reference to radio telephony it means the number of electrical vibrations per second required to produce a certain sound. In electric currents 100 per second is a low frequency current, 100,000 per second is spoken of as high frequency. In early experiments with radio telephony it was found that the chief difficulty lay in obtaining a current of sufficiently high frequency to transmit the human voice, the currents used in wireless telephony being much too weak for this purpose.

"I had, therefore, to invent my own alternator, which is attached to that gasoline motor. There is a similar one in the shed from which you just talked with me."

"But why does radio telephony require a stronger current than wireless telegraphy?" Tom wanted to know.

"Because, up to the present, no way has been found of utilizing in radio telephony the entire energy of the electric waves sent out," replied Professor Chadwick. "Only the variations in the waves can be detected, or transformed into sound at the receiving end of a radio telephone system. Therefore an immense amount of electrical energy has to be manufactured in order that the voice vibrations may register their variations as powerfully as possible."

"What percentage of the electrical energy manufactured by a high frequency alternator can be transformed into variations of sound?" asked Jack.

"Not more than five to eight per cent. of the total energy. So therefore the waste is enormous. In wireless telegraphy, on the other hand, the entire energy radiated from a sending station can be picked up to the limit of the receiver's capacity to detect it."

"Isn't there any way in which this difficulty could be overcome?" inquired Tom.

"Yes, there is," said Mr. Chadwick, after a moment's thought, "and I believe that I am the only man in the world employed with radio telephonic problems who knows of it."

"Why can't you use it, then?" asked Jack.

"Because there are almost insurmountable difficulties in the way. There is a substance chemically known Z. 2. X. which, if it could be applied to purposes of transmission and detection, has such immense powers of electrical absorption that messages could be sent almost any distance, and with far greater economy of power than at present."

"How far can you send them now?" asked Jack.

"About five miles. At least I think so. I'm not even sure of that," was Mr. Chadwick's reply.

But Jack was impatient to get back to Z. 2. X.

"Why can't you use this Z. 2. X.," he questioned, "if it would practically wipe out your troubles in sending and receiving?"

"Because there is even less of it in the world than there is of radium," was the startling reply. "At present Z. 2. X. costs far more than radium. It is the most intensely radio-active stuff in the world. It is capable of being wrought into metal if anybody had ever found enough of it, but except for a small deposit in South Africa, which has been devoted to experimental purposes, nobody has any.

"But enough of that now. That is only a dream. I am anxious, though, to test out my present apparatus thoroughly, and to do it I shall need the help of you boys."

"In what way?" asked Jack.

"In giving it a thorough trial to ascertain over how great a space I can transmit wireless speech."

"Are you going to put up another station outside the grounds?" asked Tom.

"No; I don't want to attract attention to my experiments. You boys have a wireless telegraph outfit on your Wondership?"

Jack nodded. He was curious, as was Tom, to know the Professor's plan. They did not have long to wait.

"I wish you would get the machine ready to install a radio-telephone outfit in its place. In that way I can gauge the limits of my invention without attracting undue attention, as everybody in this vicinity has seen you in flight and would imagine that you were merely taking a trip through the air."

"But can you get out an apparatus light enough for us to take up?" asked Jack.

"I am working on that now," said Mr. Chadwick. "I'll have it ready in a week."

"We'll be ready for you," promised Jack.

CHAPTER VII

THE GREAT TEST

A week later to the day on a sunshiny, windless morning, the Wondership was run out of its shed, glistening with new paint and with every bit of bright work burnished till it shone and sparkled like newly-minted silver. Amidships on the craft, the general construction of which is familiar to readers of foregoing volumes of this series, was a square metal box with small wires leading to long copper wires stretched from end to end of the Wondership's body.

These long copper wires were to form the aerials by which the messages from Mr. Chadwick's workshop were to be caught. The smaller wires underneath were connected with the metal work of the engine. These wires formed a "ground" similar to the kind employed in aerial wireless telegraphy.

The details of the Wondership having been fully described in the Boy Inventors' Flying Ship, we shall not enter here into any but a brief and general description of the craft. The Wondership, then, was a combination of dirigible balloon, automobile and boat. Her motive power was furnished by engines driven by an explosive volatile gas which was also used when occasion arose to inflate the bag of the balloon feature of her design. The gas was generated in the lower part of the craft's semi-cylindrical metal body.

On land two big aerial propellers, geared to the engine, drove the Wondership swiftly along on four solid-tired wheels. When it was desired to take to the air the balloon bag, which was neatly folded on a framework supported by upright stanchions above the body of the car, was inflated by turning on a valve connecting with the gas tanks in the base of the body.

When the Wondership was intended to navigate the water she was driven by the same aerial propellers that afforded her motive power on land or in the air. She then became what may be called a hydromobile. If it chanced to be rough weather, special hermetically sealed panels could be drawn together, completely enclosing the body and making the craft a watertight "bottle." Ventilation was provided in such a case by a hollow telescopic tube which reached twenty-five feet into the air. It was divided in two. Fresh air was drawn by a fan down one section, while the stale air in the "cabin" was forced out by a similar device up the other part of the tube. Stability was afforded by hollow pontoons, which worked on toggle joints, and could be raised or lowered as desired.

With the aid of Jupe, the gas bag was inflated to a point where only a slight additional quantity of gas would cause the craft to shoot upward to the sky. When all was ready a test of the instruments was made and they were found to be working perfectly. The powerful alternator on the Wondership was, of course, worked by the same motor that drove the big propellers.

"Well, I guess there's nothing to keep you back now," said Mr. Chadwick, who looked pale and ill after his long days and nights of work on his invention.

"No, we're as ready as we ever will be," said Jack, making ready to climb into the machine above which the big yellow balloon bag was billowing and sending impatient quiverings through the Wondership.

"I want you to promise me one thing, dad," said Jack, when he had climbed into the driver's seat, in front of Tom, whose duty it was to look after the engine.

"What is that, my boy?" asked the inventor.

"That after this test, whatever the result may be, you will take a long rest."

"Yes, I will, I must," agreed his father. "I've been working too hard, I guess, but in the excitement of perfecting the radio telephone I hardly noticed it. But recently I've had dizzy spells."

"Two weeks' rest will make you well," declared Jack, as he adjusted the controls.

"Good-by and good luck," said his father.

Both boys waved their hands.

"All ready, Tom?" hailed Jack.

The other boy nodded and then turned on a valve so that with a hissing sound additional gas rushed into the bag. Jack pulled a lever. The big motors roared and a queer, sickly smell of burned gas filled the air. The propellers began to revolve slowly and then increased their speed till they became a mere blur.

"Dere she go! Gollyumption, dere she go!" cried Jupe, capering about.

As the old black spoke, the Wondership shot up like a rocket, tilting her nose slightly into the air. But the next moment Jack had her on an even keel. In an incredibly short space of time those watching below saw her only as a glinting, golden speck against the blue sky, circling like some strange bird far above their heads.

"Now for the tests," said Mr. Chadwick, as he hastened to his workshop.

He set the big alternator at work at top speed. It droned like a gaunt bee. The inventor's face, worn by his anxious vigils at his experiments, was as keen as a hawk's, while he adjusted the instruments and placed his long, lean fingers on the tuning device.

Far above the earth Jack and Tom could look down upon a patchwork of villages, farms, green pastures, yellow grain fields and stretches of woodland. They were too far up to distinguish figures, but they could see the white steam of rushing trains along the railroad tracks, and even catch the sound of the engines' whistles.

Beyond glinted the blue of the sea flecked with sails and with here and there a steamer's smoke smudging the horizon. Both lads were in high spirits. It seemed good to be navigating the air again. Every now and then inquisitive, high-flying crows would swoop toward the machine and then dash off again with alarmed squawks.

Although they were making a high rate of speed, they hardly seemed to be moving as they soared in long circles. To get a sense of rapid motion, stationary objects must be in sight. In the lonely air it was hard to tell that they were moving at all except by looking down at the earth which, as they rose, appeared to be rushing from them, as if it were sinking through space.

But novel as all these sensations would be to an aerial novice, they were an old story to the boys. Jack devoted his attention to testing a new steering appliance he had equipped the craft with, and Tom watched his engines with an eagle eye to detect a skip or a "knock."

"How high now?" asked the young engineer after an interval.

Jack glanced at the barograph on the dashboard in front of him.

"Three thousand feet," he said.

"Might as well connect the alternator?" said Tom interrogatively.

Jack nodded, and Tom threw a lever which brought the generator of high frequency currents in contact with the motor by means of a friction fly-wheel. The alternator began to buzz and spark, crackling viciously.

A sort of metal helmet with two receivers attached to it, one on each side, lay handy at Jack's hand. In front of him was the transmitter joined to the metal box which contained the microphone, transformers and inductance tuning coil. Tuning in the aerial apparatus was effected by means of a small knob projecting through a slit in the metal box enclosing the delicate instruments including the detector. By working this knob the tuning block was moved up and down the coil till a proper "pitch" was obtained.

Jack experienced an odd thrill as he prepared to send the first spoken word ever exchanged between an airship in motion and a station on land. He and Tom had sent plenty of wireless messages while soaring through the ether, but somehow, the dot and dash system had not half the fascination and mystery of the possibility of exchanging coherent speech between land and air.

He placed his lips close to the receiver, and with his hand on the tuning knob sent forth a loud, clear hail:

"Hullo, High Towers!"

There was no answer for a few seconds while he patiently adjusted the tuning knob. But then came a faint buzz like the humming of a drowsy bee. Suddenly, sharp and distinct, as if his father was at his elbow, came Mr. Chadwick's voice in reply:

"Hullo!"

"This is the Wondership. Three thousand feet in the air," cried Jack.

"Congratulations, my boy. It's a success so far."

"What shall we do now?" asked Jack.

"I want you to fly in the direction of Rayburn, and try to keep in communication all the way."

"All right, dad," responded Jack, and altered the course of the Wondership.

Rayburn was a small village some twenty-five miles to the north of Nestorville. Jack kept the receivers on his ears as he flew along. From time to time he exchanged conversation with his father. So far everything appeared to be working as if there were no limit to the distance over which the voices from the air and land could converse.

But suddenly there came a startling interruption to the experiments.

Jack felt a sharp "Bang" at his ears as if a small cannon had been fired close at hand.

CHAPTER VIII

TALKING THROUGH SPACE

As the distance increased between air and land stations, the currents became stronger, and frequent tuning was necessary. But Jack was able to keep up a constant conversation with his father, telling him all the details of the country as they flew along. The sudden explosion, however, for it sounded like nothing else, startled him into a sharp exclamation.

"What in the world was that?"

As if he had spoken the question to someone close at hand, came back the explanation.

"Wireless telegraph wave crossing ours," said his father. "Some powerful land station is sending out a message, possibly to some ship."

"It almost broke my ear drum," said Jack, and inwardly resolved to devote some time to trying to solve the problem of avoiding such "collisions" in the future. It occurred to him that some sort of a circuit breaker might be devised to cut off, temporarily, the telephone talk by automatic means when a cross-wave of high energy struck its current.

The shock was not repeated, and the conversation went on, still as sharp and as clear as when they had started out. A few minutes later Jack was able to report they were passing over Rayburn.

"You'd better keep on," said his father, his voice aglow with enthusiasm. "It's working beyond my wildest expectations."

"It's dandy," agreed Jack.

They talked without raising their voices to any great extent, but it was necessary to articulate very clearly so that each variation of sound might be sent out into space as clearly as the notes of a singer come from the record of a phonograph. But it was amazing, almost uncanny to Jack that such results could be obtained at all.

"Goodness, if only we could get that mineral substance that dad was talking about I believe you could rig up a radio telephone that would talk across the ocean," he said to Tom, "and think what that would mean. For instance, instead of bothering with the cable you could step into a radio-telephone office and say: 'Give me the London Exchange.' In a few minutes the central would answer and you could tell her what number you wanted on some regular wire line. Before long you'd get it, and be talking to whoever you had called just as if they were twenty-five miles off instead of three thousand!"

"It seems like a dream," said Tom.

"Not much of a dream about it. All it needs is development. We've proved to-day it can be done," declared Jack, bubbling over with enthusiasm.

They flew over meadow land and pasture, farmhouses where tiny figures emerged from buildings and looked up at them, over rivers and railroads, and still the alternator spat and sparked and the messages between Jack and his father were interchanged in a steady stream. Rayburn had been left behind. They were now over a small town Jack believed to be Hempstead.

He looked at his map to make sure. It was one that he had specially plotted out himself from observations he had made when flying in the vicinity. Having verified their whereabouts he found that they had flown about fifty miles, possibly a fraction more.

But at this juncture he noticed that the voice of his father pulsing through space began to grow thin and weak. Obviously the limit of the radio 'phone's capacity had been reached.

"Better turn back," said Mr. Chadwick.

Jack turned to Tom and gave him the necessary instructions. Then he set over his guiding wheel, turning the big rudder at the stern of the Wondership and she acted as obediently as a sea-going craft answering her helm. Never had she behaved better.

They flew swiftly back toward High Towers and were soon in sight of Rayburn. In order to test what effect the magnetism of the earth had upon the radio messages, Jack brought the great flying craft close to the ground. They almost grazed the treetops as they flew along.

Skimming a patch of trees they roared above a farmhouse with a great red barn adjoining it. The barn attracted Jack's attention because of the fact that it had a flat roof, an almost unique feature in that part of the country. He supposed it was used to dry some sort of produce on and noted that there were several hop-fields near at hand. Undoubtedly the roof was used for exposing them to the sun and thus drying the moisture from them without the expense of wood for the drying fires usually used for the purpose.

He had hardly noted all this when there came a sudden tug at the Wondership as if a titanic hand had reached up from below and grasped her. She pitched wildly and, but for Jack's skill as an airman, there might have been a serious accident.

But he brought the big craft under control by skillful manipulation.

The next instant he discovered what had occurred. The grapple of the aircraft had, in some way, dropped from its fastenings and, trailing behind the Wondership, had caught in the roof of the farmer's barn.

A great section of it was torn away and as Jack brought the Wondership to rest on the roof, the only available place, for the rope was in danger of fouling the propellers if he descended to the ground, the farmer and a number of his men came running from the farmhouse.

In the hands of the farmer was a formidable looking shotgun. As the Wondership settled on the roof of the barn the man began shouting angrily.

CHAPTER IX

THE BOYS FACE TROUBLE

"Phew! looks as if we are in for trouble," exclaimed Tom, as he saw the warlike expression on the farmer's face.

"It does that," agreed Jack. "Hop out, will you, Tom, and get that grapple clear? Confound it, I don't see how it came loose."

"Wore through the lashing," said Tom, who had been examining the place where the big hooked steel anchor was usually tied.

"We ought to have seen to it before we started out," said Jack. "We haven't had it loose since that time we anchored above the Brazilian forest."

The farmer's angry voice hailed them from below.

"Hey there! Don't yew move a foot till we've had a reck'nin."

"I am awfully sorry," said Jack. "It was an accident you see. We—"

"Don't care what it was. Thet thar was a new roof. Don't you move a step till Si here gits ther constabule."

"We'll pay you for the roof," said Jack apologetically. "After all it isn't much damaged."

Indeed it appeared as if the damage was not so great as they had at first imagined. After tearing off some shingles the grapple had caught in a beam and was prevented from doing further harm.

"Yes, yew'll pay, and yew'll go ter jail tew," declared the farmer. "Consarn it all, what's the country comin' tew? Las' week tew pesky dod-ratted balloonists hit Hi Holler on ther head with a bag of sand, and now yew come along in thet thar contraption and try to bust up my dryin' roof. I'll have ther law on yer."

Matters began to look serious. Jack had no doubt but what the farmer would accept a money payment for the damaged roof. But it appeared that the old fellow was bent on more stringent vengeance.

In the meantime Tom had been busy in the stern of the craft and had succeeded in getting the grapnel loose from the beam into which its sharp points had dug. It was not till that moment that the farmer observed him.

He leveled his shotgun at the balloon of the Wondership.

"Don't yew dare ter move er I'll bust a hole right plumb through that ther airbag of yourn," he said.

"Can't you be reasonable?" asked Jack. "Here's my name." He wrote his name and address on a slip of paper and threw it down.

But the irate farmer paid no attention to the missive. He kept his gun steadily trained on the Wondership.

"Move an' I'll bust yer!" he said grimly.

A buggy drove out of the yard. It raced through the gate and then struck the highroad leading to Rayburn.

"Thar' goes Si arter ther constabule," said the farmer, licking his thin lips as if with relish. "Hi Ketchum is a rare one arter automobubblists. I reckon he'll be right smart tickled to death when he hears I got a whole airship fer him ter 'rest."

"Bother the old grouch," muttered Tom, as he climbed back into the Wondership, the bag of which was deflated just enough to keep her at rest on the roof.

"He's evidently mighty serious in his intentions," said Jack, with a troubled face. "What are we going to do?"

There was a sudden puff of wind and the big yellow balloon bag swayed slightly.

Instantly the farmer's finger crooked on his trigger. He thought the boys were going to give him the slip.

"No you don't," he shouted, "you don't fool Ezry Perkins that 'er way!"

"We're not trying to fool you," said Jack disgustedly. "Why can't you be sensible. You've our names and addresses on that paper I threw down to you. If you like I'll make a cash settlement right here for any damage we've done."

"I'm goin' ter git yer in ther court," insisted the farmer sullenly. "Las' week some autermobubblists killed three uv my chickens, week afore thet I had a hog knocked off ther road. I'm er goin' ter git even on yer fer ther lot uv them."

It was plain that the man was not to be moved by promises or persuasion. He had conceived in his mind a hatred against automobiles, with which, in a vague way, he classed airships and all such modern inventions. Jack thought, too, that Ezra Perkins was the kind of man who liked to shine out among his neighbors, and what better opportunity could he have to satisfy this ambition than by blossoming forth as a man who, single handed, had captured a great aircraft?

The boys looked down. The farmer was pacing grimly up and down like a sentry, his eyes never leaving the Wondership.

"I'd like to drop a bag of ballast on his head, the same as those balloonists did on Si's," muttered Tom.

"Wouldn't do any good," said Jack. "It would only bounce off again."

"I guess it would at that," agreed Tom with a grin.

"I've half a mind to take a chance," said Jack suddenly.

"And get a hole blown in the balloon bag," protested Tom. "We wouldn't be better off than before in that case."

"I wonder if he'd really shoot or if he's only bluffing," mused Jack.

"Take a look at him," advised Tom.

Jack did. One glance was enough. There was no bluffing about the grim, overalled farmer. The very way in which he held his gun expressed positive determination not to let the boys escape.

But as it so happened, by no action of the boys', matters were suddenly brought to a sharp crisis. Over the patch of woods beyond the farm there came a vagrant puff of wind. It was followed by a sharper gust.

The Wondership swayed and then, before Jack could check the motion, drifted off the roof like a piece of thistledown blown by the wind. Instinctively, to check the downward motion, Jack's hand sought the gas valve. With a hiss the volatile vapor rushed into the bag.

The big aircraft shot up like an arrow. For a second the farmer stood paralyzed at the suddenness of it all. His farm hands lounged about, gaping and looking upward like country folks at a fireworks display.

Then, without any warning:

"Bang!"

The farmer let loose with both barrels at once. But the Wondership still rose.

All at once, from below, came a yell of surprise and terror. The boys looked over the side. As they did so they uttered simultaneous gasps of consternation.

The trailing grapnel, for Tom had forgotten to tie it back in place in the excitement, had caught the farmer by the waistband of his overalls and he was being carried skyward by the Wondership, dangling at the end of the anchor rope like some sprawling spider.

His wife, screaming at the top of her voice, rushed from the kitchen door.

"Hey, you come back with my husband!" she shouted.

"Lemme go! Lemme go!" bawled the farmer as loudly as he could, for, held securely by his stout overalls, he was carried high above his own buildings. He kicked and struggled furiously.

"Keep still," shouted Jack, in serious alarm, from the side of the Wondership. "Keep still or you'll kick yourself off."

The farmer had sense enough to obey. He hung upside down like a limp scarecrow, while his farm hands gaped up at him and the hired girl was busy pouring buckets of water over his wife who was in hysterics.

"Gracious, now we've done it!" gasped Tom in dismay.

CHAPTER X

AN INVOLUNTARY AERONAUT

"Steady, Tom, steady," warned Jack, as he set the pumps to work drawing gas from the bag into the reservoir.

The Wondership, her buoyancy thus diminished, began to descend.

"What are you going to do?" asked Tom.

"Drop our passenger," said Jack, with a grin he could not suppress, for the struggling farmer was within a few feet of the ground now and even if he did kick himself loose, for his struggles had begun again, he could not have hurt himself much.

"Back up till we get over that haystack," said Jack, "and then play out rope till we lower him. It'll make a nice soft jumping-off place."

Tom obeyed, pulling a reverse lever. The Wondership, steered with skill by Jack's practiced hand, backed slowly up. At length they hung directly over the haystack. Jack turned and nodded. Tom sprang to the rope and lowered the indignant farmer into the soft hay. The man lost no time in disentangling himself. Then he sprang to his feet and began hurling vituperation at them at the top of his lungs.

"I'll have ther law on yer fer this," he yelled. "Tryin' ter kidnap me and bustin' down my barn. I'll see whether such goin's on is allowed in ther sufferin' state uv Massachusetts, yew see if I don't, consarn yer. I'll—"

But the Wondership, bearing the two boys who could not help laughingheartily, although they feared serious consequences might come of the accident, was winging its way onward out of earshot of the not unnaturally indignant Ezra Perkins.

They passed Rayburn before Jack noticed a peculiar smell in the atmosphere.

It was leaking gas. Then, for the first time, he recollected that the farmer might have hit the gas bag above them with his double shots, although, till then, there had been no indication that such was the case.

He called Tom to the wheel, explaining his suspicions and clambered out on the rigging to see if he could find any holes in the balloon. It would have made a less steady boy dizzy and sick to stand on the edge of the Wondership, clinging to one of the supports that held the body of the craft to the gas-bag, while the whole affair plunged and swayed five hundred feet above the earth. But Jack, used as he was to navigating the air, felt none of these qualms.

His suspicions were speedily confirmed. There was a jagged hole in the underbody of the balloon, from which gas was rushing. Jack's face grew grave. The situation was dangerous.

He knew, as does every balloonist, that out-rushing gas can make an electric spark in the atmosphere which, in turn, ignites the gas itself, sometimes with fatal results. Experts in aeronautics attribute the disasters befalling the long series of Zeppelins, the giant German dirigibles, to this cause.

"Tom, we must go down. Drop at once," he said. "That old fellow succeeded in blowing a hole in us all right."

The pumps were set to work and the Wondership fell rapidly. They dropped in a field by the roadside, landing on the running wheels as lightly as a feather, thanks to the shock absorbers, similar to those of an automobile, with which the Wondership was equipped.

"Now for the repair kit," said Jack, rummaging a locker.

He soon had balloon silk, big shears, a quick-drying gum solution and a pot of gasproof varnish, ready for the job of patching up the hole. But first they had to empty the big bag of gas. This was speedily done, for already enough had escaped to wrinkle the bag like a walnut, with hollows and creases.

Jack cut out a patch of balloon silk large enough to fit the hole and spread it with the adhesive gum solution. This he placed inside the hole, spreading it out so that when pressure was applied it would be pressed firmly against the aperture. Then he coated the patch with the gasproof varnish, and both boys sat down to give the job time to "set."

Their eyes turned idly to the high-road. It was about noon and there was a heavy sort of silence in the air. Far on the horizon they could make out great billowy masses of white cloud. Piled and castellated against the sky they assumed all kinds of odd shapes.

"Thunder heads," said Jack. "We shall have a storm before to-night."

"It's sultry enough for anything," said Tom, taking off his cap and mopping his forehead. "I'd hate to be walking in this weather like that fellow yonder."

A man had come into sight, plodding along with bent head and eyes on the ground as if he was very tired. The gray dust of the road coated him from head to foot. He walked with a kind of dragging gait.

Over his shoulder he carried some sort of a bundle on a stick. His hat was a broad sombrero, like a cowboy's. It was a kind of headgear seldom seen in the east and attracted the boys' attention. Round the man's neck was a red handkerchief, the only spot of color on his dust-covered person. He had a great yellow beard and rather long, unkempt hair.

"Tramp," hazarded Tom.

Jack shook his head.

"Doesn't look like that to me somehow," he said. "I rather think—"

Round the corner whizzed a big red automobile. It was coming fast. The driver, a young man, had his head turned and was talking to three companions who sat in the tonneau. He did not see the dusty traveler in the road ahead.

The boys set up a shout.

"Look out! you'll run him down. Look out—"

But their caution came too late. At top speed the auto struck the wayfarer, and before the boys' horrified eyes he was thrown high in the air, to fall, a confused sprawl of legs and arms, at the wayside.

CHAPTER XI

BY THE ROADSIDE

The boys ran forward across the few yards of meadow that intervened between the Wondership and the roadway. The autoists did not, apparently, notice them. They had stopped the car and were looking back.

"Come on and let's get out of this quick," one of them, a hawk-faced youth, with a long motoring duster on, was shouting to the driver.

"Yes, let's beat it while the going's good, Bill," came from his companion as he addressed the driver of the car.

"I guess we'd better," said the man addressed as Bill.

Before the boys could intervene the car was on its way again, at top speed, leaving the unconscious form of its victim at the roadside.

"Of all the cold-blooded scoundrels!" gasped Jack, horrified at such callousness.

"Never mind them now," advised Tom. "Let's see if this poor fellow is badly hurt. He may even be—"

He did not finish the sentence, but Jack knew what he meant. Hastily the boys scrambled down the low bank that separated the field from the road. They ran quickly to the man's side. To their great relief, for they had feared that he might have been killed, the man was breathing. But his breath came pantingly from his parted lips and there was a bad cut on his forehead.

"Get some water from the creek yonder," said Jack, and Tom hastened up the road to where, beneath the small wooden bridge, there flowed a rivulet of water.

He was soon back, with his handkerchief well soaked, and with an old can, that he had been lucky enough to find, filled with water. They bathed the man's wound and then bound it up as best they could. But he still lay senseless.

"Now what's to be done?" asked Tom.

"We ought to get him over to the Wondership and rush him to the hospital at Nestorville," said Jack.

"Yes, that would be the thing to do. But he's too heavy for us to carry," objected Tom.

"Why not fly over here alongside him. I guess we could lift him in; that patch ought to hold by this time," suggested Jack.

"That's a good idea. What a pack of cowardly sneaks those chaps in that car were."

"I wish we could have stopped them. It would give me real pleasure to see a gang like that get its just deserts. They might have killed this poor fellow."

The unconscious man was powerfully built, with face tanned brown above a yellow beard, from exposure to sun and wind. As Jack had said, he did not look like a tramp. Suddenly the boy noticed lying near him an object which had evidently fallen from the man's pocket when he was struck and flung through the air by the auto.

It was a small cylinder, apparently made of lead, and about three inches long. Jack picked it up, and for the time being did not attempt to examine it but thrust it into his pocket for safe keeping. Little did either of the boys think how much that little cylinder was to mean to them, and how it was to influence some of the most important adventures of their lives.

Making the man as comfortable as they could, by rolling up their coats and placing them under his head, the boys hurried back to the Wondership. When they arrived there they saw that a feature of the radio 'phone, which has not yet been mentioned, was working in urgent appeal. This was a tiny red electric light attached to the top of the case containing the sensitive parts of the apparatus.

By an ingenious device, worked as a call signal from the transmitting station, the electric waves converted a lighting circuit for this purpose.

It was winking and twinkling, and Jack knew that his father was trying to call them.

He sent out some flashes by starting the dynamo going and pressing a key devised for the purpose. This, he knew, would cause a similar light attached to his father's apparatus to flash a reply. This done he waited a second and then adjusted the receivers to his ears.

"What's the matter?" came his father's voice.

Jack gave him a rapid account of the accident, not stopping just then to say anything about the incident of the farmer and his barn.

"What are you going to do about it?" asked his father.

"He appears to be seriously hurt," said Jack. "I was thinking of rushing him to the hospital at Nestorville."

"That seems to be the best plan," said his father. "By the way, did those autoists get clear away?"

"I'm afraid so. They never even waited a second to see if the man was badly injured. They—"

Jack suddenly stopped short. An inspiration had come to him. The accident had happened on a road that, as he knew, led straight through Nestorville. He had thought of a plan to bring the autoists to book for their callousness and negligence.

"Dad—oh, dad!" he called.

"Yes, what is it?" came back Mr. Chadwick's voice.

"Those fellows will pass through Nestorville. I had a flash of the number of the car. It was 4206 Mass. It's a red car and a powerful one, with three men in it."

"What do you want to do?" asked Mr. Chadwick.

"Can't you 'phone to the Nestorville police, telling them what has happened and have those fellows stopped. I'm not vindictive, but they ought to be brought to book for running down a man and then speeding off and leaving him like that."

"I agree with you," replied Mr. Chadwick. "I'll do so at once. Good-by."

"Good-by," said Jack and "rang off."

"That was a great idea of yours, Jack, old boy," approved Tom. "I hope they land those fellows."

"Of course it was an accident," said Jack, "but that fellow who was driving was too busy talking to watch the road, and then going off like that—they deserve all they get."

Examination of the patch showed that it would hold fast and

the bag was refilled. As soon as it was sufficiently inflated, the Wondership sailed over to the road and was brought down alongside the still unconscious man.

"Looks as if he's badly hurt," said Tom with some anxiety.

"It does. His skull may be fractured," agreed Jack. "If he is seriously injured those fellows may get into trouble."

It required all the boys' strength to raise the man and get him into the Wondership. Here they laid him out on the floor of the rear section. They had just done this when the red light signaled Jack again. It was Mr. Chadwick. He had notified the Nestorville police force, consisting of a chief and two men, and they were on the lookout for the offending auto.

"Good," said Jack. "Say, dad, the radio telephone has shown its usefulness on the first day out, hasn't it?"

They were soon in the air once more. The run to Nestorville was made quickly. On the outskirts of the town they came to earth and deflated the balloon bag, since the hospital stood in a group of trees and it would have been impossible to make a landing there. The Wondership was converted into an auto and sent speeding toward the main street of the village.

Suddenly they heard a whir of wheels behind them and an impatient tooting of a horn. They looked back and uttered a simultaneous cry of astonishment.

The red auto that had run down the yellow-bearded man was behind them. Its occupants were shouting and sounding their horn impatiently for the right of way.

CHAPTER XII

MAKING ENEMIES

The road was narrow where they were, and unless the boys' machine was run to one side of the road there was no chance for the red machine to pass. Jack made it clear that he didn't intend to let them.

He paid no attention to the shouts that came from behind.

"Hey, you kids, with that queer-looking car, get off the road and give a real machine a chance to get by," shouted the driver, he who had been addressed as Bill.

Jack did not turn his head.

"I'll knock your head off if you don't turn out—and turn out quick!" came another shout.

Still the boys did not pay any attention. In this order they came into Nestorville. Lined up, with a look of stern determination on his face, and with his nickel star of office newly polished, was Chief Biff Bivins. Behind him were Lena Hardy and Joe Curley, his "force."

"Say, boys," hailed Chief Biff, as the boys rolled up abreast of him and his men, "hain't seen hair nor hide of that car your dad was arter 'phonin' me about."

"Well, you soon will, chief," said Jack.

"Haow do yew know that?" asked the chief, his little eyes blinking curiously.

"Because it's right behind us now," declared Jack. "It's that red one."

"Ther dickens you say. How'd you come ter git erhead of 'em?"

"They must have stopped to fix a tire or something," said Jack.

But Biff was paying no attention to him. The majesty of the law was strong upon him. Calling his minions to his side he stepped into the middle of the road in front of the red car.

"Get out of the way!" shouted the man who was driving.

"Not much I won't," declared Biff valorously. "Halt that gasoline gadabout o' yourn instanter."

"What for, you old Rube?"

"Old Rube am I?" sputtered Biff, feeling that the law had been insulted in his person, "jes' fer thet yer under 'rest."

"What for?" demanded the driver of the red car angrily.

"Fer running daown and grievously wounding a man and then speedin' off without stoppin' ter see if you'd killed him dead or what all. That's what fer."

The driver of the red machine lost his blustering tone.

"Why, there's some mistake," he stammered, his face very pale, "I—er—we—er—that is, we didn't run anybody down."

"Oh, yes, you did," said Jack. "We saw you, and what's more

we've got the man you struck right here in our car. You're a fine pack of cowards to run off like that. If we hadn't happened along he might have lain there for hours before help came."

"You saw us!" gasped the driver of the car, losing his bravado completely. "Well, I might as well admit we did run a man down. But we didn't think he was badly hurt and so we put on all speed to rush into town here and get a doctor for him. We'd have been here sooner only one of our tires punctured."

"Thet's a dern good story," said the chief, "but you'll hev ter 'splain that ter ther squire. Come on with me ter ther courthouse. Too bad fer you thet them Chadwick boys had some sort of a do-funny dingus on their sky buggy that talks through the air, otherwise you'd hev got clar' away."

The man had, by this time, got out of the car which they halted at the side of the street. A crowd of curious villagers gathered and were staring at the scene and the actors in it.

At Chief Biff's words the driver of the red car flashed an angry look at the boys. His companions looked equally vindictive.

"So, it's to you we owe our arrest, is it?" he said in a low voice, coming quite close to Jack. "All right. You'll hear from me later. I'm not going to forget you or that other kid, either. Do you understand?"

Jack made no reply, and as he was anxious to get the injured man to the hospital as quickly as possible he drove off. At the institution the man was carried to a cot by two orderlies, and the doctor in charge told the boys that, so far as he could see, his injuries were not mortal, although he added that a fracture of the skull was possible.

"In which case," he said, "his recovery is problematical. How did you happen to pick him up?" asked the doctor, who knew the boys quite well.

Jack told him as briefly as he could, and received the physician's warm congratulations.

"It was fortunate that you happened along," he said. "Otherwise a long exposure to the sun, unattended, might have resulted in the man's death. Have you any idea who he is?"

"Not the least," replied Jack. "All that we know is that, just after he had plodded round the corner as if he was tired after walking a long way, that auto came whizzing round and struck him. Somehow he doesn't look like a tramp."

"No, he doesn't," agreed the doctor. "However, he should be conscious to-morrow if there are no complications, and we can find out. One thing is certain, he ought to be grateful to you."

"Oh, that's all right," laughed Jack, much relieved to hear that the man wasn't going to die. "It was all we could do."

They drove back through the village. Outside the court-house was quite a crowd. Events were few and far between in sleepy Nestorville, and the arrest of the autoists had caused quite a sensation. From a friend in the crowd the boys learned that the three men were being arr aigned before Squire Stevens.

"Let's go in," suggested Tom.

"All right," nodded Jack, and they climbed out of the Wondership and ascended the long steps leading into the court-house. As they entered Squire Stevens' court-room, Chief Bivins spied them.

"Here they be now, Squire," he said. "Glad you came, boys. It saved me the trouble of serving subpoenas on you. These are the boys who saw the whole thing, judge."

"Was it an accident?" asked Squire Stevens, a dignified-looking old man with an imposing white beard.

"Yes, entirely so," said Jack, who did not bear any malice.

"But after they had struck the man, these young men ran away?"

"Yes," Jack was forced to admit. The men shot him a glance of hatred.

"I understand you have been to the hospital," went on Squire Stevens. "Did you learn how badly the man they hit is hurt?"

"The doctor told us that his injuries don't appear to be serious," said Jack, "but that it was possible there might be complications."

"In that case I shall have to hold you young men under bond," said the squire. "Will you be able to furnish it?"

"In any amount," said the man who had driven the car, in a loud, boastful voice. "My father, Evans Masterson, owns the *Boston Moon,* the evening paper. If I can telephone to him he will soon get us out of this scrape."

"Very well, then," said the Squire, frowning slightly at young Masterson's tone. "I shall fix your bond at $500, as you were driving the car and directly responsible for the accident, and that of your companions at $100 each."

Young Masterson gave an ironical bow. Chief Biff Bivins escorted him to the telephone. The elder Masterson, who had had a good deal of experience with his son's escapades, at first administered a lecture over the 'phone which ended by his saying that he would come post-haste to Nestorville and extricate his son and his chums from their unpleasant fix.

But the boys did not wait for this. As soon as the case was over they hastened back to the Wondership. The run home was made without incident and it was not till the Wondership was safely in its shed that Jack suddenly thought of the odd cylinder of lead that he had picked up by the man's side as he lay on the road.

"I ought to have left it at the hospital," he thought, "but I entirely forgot it."

He drew it out and looked at it. He now saw that the lead cylinder enclosed a glass vial carefully corked and sealed. The bottle was wrapped in flannel. Jack could not withstand the temptation of pulling it out and looking at it. He hardly knew what he had expected to see, but he was distinctly disappointed, as was Tom, to find that the carefully protected vial contained nothing more than some dark, almost black, stuff that looked like sand. In it were particles that glittered like mica.

"Pshaw!" he exclaimed in a disappointed tone, "nothing but a bottle full of sand. Wonder why in the world that fellow carried trash like that so carefully wrapped up for?"

The solution of the question, which was near at hand, was to have an important bearing on the lives of the Boy Inventors, and that in the immediate future.

CHAPTER XIII

THE LEADEN TUBE

The following day, while they were experimenting and practicing with the radio telephone, the boys received word that the man in the hospital was conscious and wished to see them, if possible.

"Perhaps now we shall get some explanation of that queer tubeful of sand," said Jack, as he hung up the telephone receiver, having informed the physician that they would be at the hospital shortly.

"It's certainly a queer sort of thing for a man to carry about—a glass vial full of black grit so carefully protected, unless he is crazy or something," commented Tom.

"I think that there is some explanation back of all this," said Jack, "and for my part the sooner we get to the hospital, the better I shall be pleased. The man told the doctor he was a miner and his name is Zeb Cummings. Perhaps that sand is gold-bearing or something like that."

"That might be the case," agreed Tom.

The boys decided to take out the electric car. It was in perfect running order and the indicator showed that there was plenty of electricity in storage for the start. They told Mr. Chadwick where they were going and then rolled out of the High Towers gates onto the broad, smooth road bordered with pleasant green elms.

They bowled along smoothly and silently with the car working as perfectly as delicate clockwork. They had gone about a mile from the house and were on a steep grade which the car took as easily as if it had been going down hill, when their attention was attracted by a sudden shout from the vicinity.

Jack brought the car to a halt. The voice came again.

"Hi! Help me! Ouch! Help!"

"What in the world is the matter now?" wondered Tom.

"Somebody in trouble in that field yonder. We'd better get out and see what's up," proposed Jack.

The shouts seemed to issue from beyond a high bank at one side of the road. On its summit was a hedge which prevented the boys seeing what was going on in the field that lay beyond.

As they got out of the car, however, Jack spied a bicycle at one side of the road. A satchel that he remembered very well was slung from its frame.

"It's the professor in trouble again!" declared Jack.

"I do believe you are right," replied Tom as they scrambled up the bank. "That's sure enough his wheel."

They found a gate in the hedge and on the other side an odd sight met their eyes. Kneeling on the ground was the professor. His right arm was thrust almost up to the shoulder into a hole in the ground. He was shouting lustily for help and appeared to be imprisoned in his queer posture.

"Some animal has got hold of his hand," cried Jack. "Come on, Tom."

"Oh, boys, thank goodness you've come," gasped the scientist.

"What's the matter?" demanded Jack.

"I can't get my arm out of this hole," declared the professor.

"How did you get it in?" asked Tom.

"A fine specimen that I dropped accidentally rolled into it," was the reply. "I reached in to get it and now I can't get my hand out."

"But you got it in easily enough," said Jack in a puzzled tone.

"Ah, yes," replied the professor, "but then I didn't have my hand clenched. Now my fist is closed and I have the specimen in it. Oh, boys, it's a beauty. One of the finest I have ever seen. It shows distinct monolithic traces."

"But if you don't drop it you can't get your hand out," argued Tom.

"I know that. That's why I shouted for help," said the professor simply.

"You'll have to let go of it," decided Jack, almost choking with laughter at the plight of the eccentric little man.

"Let go of it? My dear sir," murmured the professor in a shocked tone, "this specimen is worth at least twenty dollars, not to speak of its scientific value."

"But you can't stay here," said Jack decisively.

"And I won't let go of the specimen," declared the professor with equal firmness.

"What on earth are we to do?" said Jack, looking helplessly at Tom.

Not far off Tom had noticed a man digging potatoes. It gave him an idea.

"We can borrow that man's shovel and dig his arm out," he suggested.

"It's about the only thing to do, I guess," said Jack. "You go and see if you can get it. I'll keep the professor company."

Tom soon came back. The potato-digger accompanied him. The man was much interested in the eccentric man's plight.

"If that ain't the beatingest I ever heard on," he remarked, gazing at the professor, and then he tapped his head significantly and looked at the boys in a knowing way.

"Nobody home, eh?" he said with a grin. Fortunately the professor did not hear him; but the boys could hardly keep from laughing outright as they set to work with the spade. A few minutes of brisk digging set the professor at liberty and he was able to stand upright and triumphantly exhibit a small black rock which looked in no way remarkable, but which, it was evident, he esteemed highly.

"Ah, my little gem," he said, gazing at it fondly. "You thought you'd escape me; but you didn't. A wonderfully fine specimen, boys."

"Tell yer what," said the yokel, from whom they had borrowed the spade, "I'll pay you fifty cents a day to clean up my back pasture yonder. It's chock full of them black rocks."

"It is?" exclaimed the professor eagerly. "I must visit it some day. It would be worth writing a paper about. Most remarkable. A whole field of these stones. Well, well, this is a great day for science. But how did you boys happen to come along so opportunely?"

Jack explained, and then, suddenly, he thought of the tube of queer-looking black sand. Possibly the professor would know what it was. He drew it out and briefly narrated how he came in possession of it. The professor took the little glass vial out of its protecting lead and flannel. He adjusted his glasses and held it up to the light. Then he uncorked it and sprinkled a few grains on the palm of his hand.

He regarded it carefully for a few minutes and then drew out a huge magnifying glass. The next instant he dropped his scientific calm and uttered a sharp exclamation of astonishment.

"Where is the man who owns this?" he exclaimed. "We must see him at once."

CHAPTER XIV

IN THE HOSPITAL

"We are on our way to see him now," said Jack. "He is in the Nestorville hospital."

"May I go with you?" asked the professor, with astonishing eagerness for him.

"Why, of course. But that black sand," said Jack. "What is it—gold-bearing material of some kind?"

"Gold!" exclaimed the professor with fine scorn, "gold would be dross beside it. Of course I haven't analyzed it yet, but if it is what I think it is, it is the most valuable stuff in the world."

The boys exchanged bewildered glances. Clearly their discovery of the injured man, Zeb Cummings, had an aspect they had not hitherto suspected. But the professor refused to tell them what the sand was, or what he thought it was, till he had seen Zeb Cummings himself.

Leaving the potato-digger under the firm impression that they were all crazy, they hurried back to the road, the professor's bicycle was placed in the tonneau, and Jack drove just within the speed law to the hospital.

They found the injured man sitting up in bed, his great yellow beard gleaming like gold. His head was bandaged but even the pallor induced by the accident had not materially altered the ruddy glow of his thick coat of tan.

"So these are the boys who saved me," he said, extending a big, gnarled hand. "Shake, pardners. The doc here tells me if I'd laid much longer out there in the sun, there might hev been a first-class funeral fer Zeb Cummings."

"Oh, that's all right," said Jack easily. "I'm only glad that we came along when we did."

"Well, you sure acted different from them other varmints," said Zeb with deep conviction. "The doc tole me all about it."

His face suddenly grew grave as he changed the subject.

"Did you find anything on the ground thereabouts after I got knocked out?" he asked.

"What sort of a thing?" asked Jack.

"Oh, nothing that looked very valuable. Jes' a little lead roll with a bottle full of what looked like black sand in it."

"Got it right here," said Jack, producing the bottle which the professor had given back to him.

"Glory be!" exclaimed Zeb Cummings, as he took the lead-wrapped vial as though it was something precious. "I was afeard that if anyone found it they might hev thrown it away, bein' as it don't look as if it amounted ter anything much."

"Is it valuable?" asked Jack, who could not restrain his curiosity.

"That's jes' what I don't rightly know," rejoined Zeb. "I reckon I'd better tell yer how I come ter git it an' then you kin judge fer yourselves."

"We'd like to hear," said Jack, who had felt all along that there was some mystery about the yellow-bearded giant.

"All right! Sit down and I'll tell yer ther yarn. But say, who is yer friend? No offense meant, ye understand."

"This is Professor Jerushah Jenks," said Jack.

"What, the guy that knows all about rocks and such like?" burst out the miner.

"I believe I have achieved some small fame in that line," said the professor.

"Wa'al if this don't beat pay dirt I'm a Piute," exclaimed the miner. "Give us your hand, Professor. I was on my way ter see you when that thar buzz wagon busted me higher nor a turkey buzzard."

"On your way to see me?" echoed the professor in amazed tones.

"Yes, siree bob, that very identical thing," was the bronzed miner's reply.

"But I don't quite understand. You see I—"

"That's all right, Professor. We'll git down ter pay dirt direc'ly," said the miner. "You know of the Scientific Society in Bosting, of course?"

"I am a member of that body, sir," was the dignified reply of the little man.

"Well, they giv' me your name. Said you was the biggest bug on rocks, minerals and sich in the country and so I sets out to pay a call on you."

"But you were many miles from where I live," said the

professor. "The railroad, or the trolley—"

"Don't carry folks for nothing," interrupted Zeb, "and nothing's my capital right now."

"You mean that you were walking from Boston?" asked the professor.

"That's right," was the reply. "Landed there on ship from round the Horn last week. Got paid off but some sneak thief in the boarding house I was stopping at got my roll. So I had to hoof it."

"But what did you want with me?" asked the professor.

"I wanted you ter tell me ef that thar stuff in the glass tube is worth anything or nothing," was the reply.

"Why, do you know where there is more of it?" asked the professor, and the boys could see that he was oddly excited, although preserving an appearance of outward calm.

"Yes, siree," was the emphatic reply. "I know whar thar's enough of it to load a freight train."

"Shades of Huxley!" gasped the professor, actually turning pale. "Do you mean that?"

"I sure do, Professor. It's all down on a map what Blue Nose Sanchez give me afore he passed in his checks."

CHAPTER XV

A TALE OF THE COLORADO

"Do you fully realize what you are telling me?" asked the professor. The doctor and the nurse had left the room, and the miner, the scientist and the boys were alone.

"Course I do," was the rejoinder of the yellow-bearded giant with the bandaged head. "There ought ter be a fortune in it 'cording to what Blue Nose Sanchez said. Was he lyin', Professor?"

"I don't think so. But tell us your story," urged the man of science.

"Well, it begins some months ago. I was prospecting down along the Colorado River. It was in a mighty bad place. Don't rightly know just how I ever got thar, but thar I was. Wonder was I wasn't killed ten times over 'fore I got to whar I was. But I guess I'm pretty tough.

"That Colorado River is a pretty tough place down where I was. Nothing but desert all around, and just a swift dashing current at the bottom of a canyon that looks like it went into the middle of the earth with steep, dark walls that seem to go straight plum up to the sky.

"But I was lured on by the thought of making a big strike. At last I got down to a place where the banks was so high and steep that it was like twilight even at noon. Grub was gittin' to be a question with me, and I'd about made up my mind to turn back, but I thought I'd make one more last try.

"I set to work on a rocky bank with my pick but nary a color—that's what we call a trace of gold—could I uncover.

"Wa'al, says I to myself, it's up stakes fer you, Zeb, unless you want to starve afore you git back to civilization. But as it was evenin' then I decided to stay whar I was that night and strike back early the next day.

"Here's whar Blue Nose Sanchez comes inter ther story. They called him 'blue nose,' I guess, because of a premature blast that had blown powder into his nose and turned it that color. Anyway, he was a mighty homely specimen.

"It was just gittin' light in the canyon, although it must have been broad day up above, when I hears an almighty hollering up the gulch. The next thing I knows, round a bend comes a small boat. There's two men in it. They must have been crazy to try to make the passage, for the river is just a mass of rapids and whirlpools, and I never heard of anyone trying to shoot 'em.

"But thar was these two fellows in this boat, and they was scared, too, I kin tell you. Wa'al, I stood thar like a stuffed pig on the bank watching 'em as they came toward me at the speed of an express train. Suddenly one of 'em, the chap that was trying to steer, twisted the oar he was guiding the boat with and it cracked under his weight. He went overboard in a flash.

"The next moment, with a yell of fright that I kin hear yit, the boat was hurried past me on that water that boiled like yeast in a kittle, and in a flash it had disappeared round another bend. What became of it I never knew, but it must have been upset and the man in it drowned. No boat could have lasted long in that water, even with an oar to steer it, and that was gone.

"I waded out inter ther water as far as I dared and by some freak of the current the man who had toppled out of the boat came within my reach. I grabbed him and dragged him ashore, more dead than alive. I done what I could for him and he came to after a while. That was how I met Blue Nose Sanchez.

"Well, sir, Blue Nose was a mighty sick man, even then. He had fever and was a ravin' lunatic at times, but at intervals he made out to tell me suthin' of his story. Him and his partner, a fellow he called Foxy Joe, was on their way to find a little island down ther river where no white man but only one had been. This man was a friend of Foxy Joe's and the two met up in Yuma. Foxy's friend had a lot to tell him about a wonderful island some Injuns had told him about whar there was some sort of mysterious mineral. By what Joe could make out this mineral was nuthin' more nor less than radium."

"Radium!" exclaimed the boys.

"That's right," went on the miner. "Foxy's friend allowed that there was cartloads of it lyin' loose thar 'cording to the description the Injuns give him, and he showed Foxy a sample of the stuff. That sample is in this little lead-wrapped bottle. It's wrapped in lead 'cos otherwise it 'ud make sores on you when you carry it about. It's workin', workin' all the time, frum what I kin make out.

"Well, 'cordin' ter ther way Blue Nose Sanchez tells it, Foxy and the man who knew about the island and had a rough plan of it the Injuns drew fer him, had a fight, and Foxy kills him, or thinks he has. Blue Nose sees it and sees Foxy take the map and the little lead-wrapped bottle off the body. He suspects somethin' and tells Foxy that he'll give him up to the law if he don't let him in on it. So Foxy tells him all about it and him and Sanchez, who was then a mule rustler, agrees ter go partners and go git ther radium, or whatever it is.

"They builds this boat, the one that disappeared, and in order that Foxy shouldn't play no tricks, that bein' his disposition,

Sanchez 'lows he'll take both the sample and the map. Foxy sees no way out of it but to give in and that's the way it's fixed.

"The boat is taken out of Yuma in sections and then put together in a place whar nobody ain't likely to come nosin' around. Then they starts out on what I guess was the most darn-fool enterprise any two locoed fortune-hunters ever undertook. How it ended you know. They both got fever, but Sanchez was the worst. He died that same evening, his tumble in the water havin' made him worse. I buried him there as best I could and then, as he had wished, I takes the sample and the map.

"Some day," he told me, just afore he closed his eyes for good, "you'll be glad you saved me, even though it was too late."

"Well, I beat it back and get out of the canyon more dead than alive and finally make a small strike. I go to San Francisco with it and try to git ther stuff analyzed, but everyone I tole about it laughed at me and said I was crazy. So, thinks I, I'll come East. My money was about all gone, so I shipped afore ther mast on a Cape Horn ship, and got here.

"Now, you have me tale, old top," grinned the good-natured miner, and added: "Well, has my toe-and-heeling been worth its salt?"

The professor nodded solemnly.

"What is it?" cried Jack, his heart beating with a strange, wild hope.

Tom and Zeb echoed Jack's eager question.

"My friends," declared the little man of science pompously, "we have reason to believe that a wonderful discovery has been made, namely, Z.2.X."

CHAPTER XVI

ZEB CUMMINGS

"Z.2.X., the most radio-active stuff in the world!" exclaimed Jack.

"I suppose that approximately describes it," said the professor, "but what do you know about it?"

Jack explained how ardently his father had wished for the missing element to make his system of radio telephony the most efficient in use.

"Well, if what Sanchez said was true, and the map is right, there is plenty of it right on that island," said the miner.

"Yes, that may all be," objected the professor, "but how are you going to get at it?"

"Wa'al that's a poser. You can't reach it in a boat and you can't reach it over the desert," said Zeb. "The country all round there is dry as an oven and, anyhow, if you got to ther banks of ther Colorado right by ther island ther's no way of gitting *down* to ther island. Sanchez says that the Injuns told Foxy's friend that a long time ago, when first they found the stuff on the island, there was a way of getting down to it. But an earthquake sunk the river bed and nobody had been thar since the Injuns that found it. He said that they first come to take notice of it by reason of the way it shined at night. But only a few of the tribe would go near on account of their thinking the place was haunted."

"Have you got that map?" asked the professor.

"Yes, if you'll reach my coat I'll show it you," said the miner.

Jack gave him the ragged garment off a hook at the back of the door. Zeb fumbled in the pockets for a minute and then brought out a knife.

"A rip more or less won't make no difference," he said, and cut a slash down the lining. There, carefully stowed inside, where it could not be suspected, was a folded, time-yellowed paper.

The miner opened it slowly and spread it out on the counterpane. The boys, not without a sense of shock, noted a dark, rusty-looking stain upon it. It struck them that the marks might be the life blood of the treacherous Foxy's friend who had met a tragic end in Yuma.

Zeb, with a broad and blackened forefinger, traced the course of the Colorado. At length his finger paused at an island marked in red. There was some fantastic Indian lettering, or sign-drawing, about it, and underneath, in a white man's handwriting, were the words: "Rattlesnake Island."

"I reckon Foxy Joe's friend must hev written that in," commented Zeb.

"It looks that way," said the professor, who had poured the sample of mineral-bearing sand back into the vial and restored it to Zeb Cummings.

"Rattlesnake Island," repeated Jack. "Are there any rattlers down that way?"

"Yes, and gila monsters and tarantulas and centipedes," replied Zeb cheerfully. "But you soon get used to 'em."

Some other islands were marked on the map, but Rattlesnake Island was the only one designated by name.

"That must be the place whar all that stuff is, then," decided Zeb. "I wish thar was some way of gittin' thar."

"If there is even only a small fraction of the mineral-bearing sand there," said the professor, "there's a fortune in it."

"Wa'al if you can't git it out what good is it?" said Zeb philosophically. "Anyhow, I'm glad that Sanchez spoke the truth with his dying words. Maybe thar is some way, except by water, in spite of what he said."

"Maybe there is," said Jack. "It seems a shame to think of all that rich stuff lying there neglected and unobtainable."

"It does indeed," agreed the professor. "In that sample I find traces of metals from which filaments for electric lights could be made and substances invaluable in medicine for X-ray purposes as well as the Z.2.X. which your father is convinced would make the radio telephone as practical as the wireless telegraph."

They would like to have stayed there all the morning poring over the map and asking further questions of the rugged miner, but at that moment the nurse came in and declared that the injured man must have quiet.

And so there, for the present, the matter rested. The professor departed for his home greatly excited over the events of the morning, but his excitement was a little allayed by the fear that he would be late for his mid-day meal with dire results from Miss Melissa.

As for the boys, they could talk of nothing else. The idea of that lonely island, lying at the bottom of an unscalable canyon in the midst of a burning, desolate desert, appealed powerfully to their imaginations. Their minds were in a whirl over the strange coincidence that had brought them in contact with a man who knew where possibly inexhaustible supplies of the mysterious Z.2.X. lay ready for the taking, provided it could be reached.

"I'd give a whole lot to be able to fix up an expedition to go out there and get that stuff," said Jack with a sigh.

"So would I," agreed Tom. "But I guess, as Zeb Cummings said, it will be a long time before anyone sets foot on Rattlesnake Island."

CHAPTER XVII

IN THE LABORATORY

That afternoon Jack broached to his father the events of the morning. Mr. Chadwick's enthusiasm may be imagined as his son told him of the professor's hasty analysis of the contents of Zeb Cumming's glass vial.

But there remained the insuperable obstacle of the remoteness of the island where the deposits lay, and the difficulties—in fact, almost the impossibilities—that barred the way. For the time being, however, the matter was set aside while further experiments with the radio telephone were conducted. As a means of increased transmitting power, Mr. Chadwick had in mind a series of sending devices attached to one mouthpiece. In this way he believed he could at least partially overcome the resistance of the atmosphere, and get a higher percentage of current.

He had been working on the idea all the morning and was anxious for a test. The Wondership was, therefore, wheeled out, and before long the boys were in the air once more. As before, they sailed in the direction of Rayburn. As they passed above the farm where they had met with their adventure the day before, they turned to each other with a laugh.

Below them they could see men working on the damaged roof of the barn and Tom burst into an uncontrollable fit of laughter as he recalled the queer sight the farmer presented dangling from the grapnel high above his broad acres.

"That reminds me," said Jack. "We must send him some money for that roof."

"How about his personal feelings?" grinned Tom.

"I guess he wiped that score out when he blazed away at the balloon bag."

"Just the same, I think we'd better go pretty high up," advised Tom. "He might fancy trying another shot at us."

"That's so," agreed Jack, studying the men moving about far below.

He pulled a lever and the Wondership began to rise. It was as well he did so perhaps, for as they shot upward they could see that their presence had been noted. They watched the men scurrying about and pointing upward. But whether the Wondership was too high, or his animosity had cooled after his involuntary ascension, the farmer made no hostile demonstration, and they were soon out of Perkins' sight.

Apparently the new device worked fine, for all through the afternoon, at various heights and distances, they kept in perfect touch with Mr. Chadwick. Every intonation of his voice was borne plainly to their ears, Tom at times taking the wheel and the receivers while Jack relieved him at the engines.

The storm which had threatened the night before, still was hovering about, as was evidenced by the white thunderheads piled on the horizon. But the electricity in the air did not, as is sometimes the case, interfere with the powerful impulses sent out from workshop and airship. Although the air felt heavy, the instruments worked perfectly.

The boys flew over hill and dale for more than seventy miles prior to any perceptible weakening in the current. But once it began to fail it reduced rapidly until the messages were scarcely audible. But the experiments were kept up till almost dusk, when Mr. Chadwick told the boys to come back.

As they returned the radio 'phones were kept working and as the distance decreased the impulses grew stronger.

"If only I had some of that Z.2.X.," said Mr. Chadwick, "I believe it would be possible to send a message across the ocean or the continent."

Not long after this Jack heard again from his father. It was a commonplace message enough. Sent merely to keep the airline in operation.

"Here is Jupe with the afternoon mail," he said.

"Anything for us?" asked Jack, enjoying the novel sensation of talking through the air concerning such everyday matters.

"Yes, there's one from Ned Nevins," was the rejoinder, "and here is one for me from my New York brokers. Let me see— ah-h-h-h!"

The last was a sharp exclamation, as if Mr. Chadwick had received a sudden shock. It was followed by silence. Again and again Jack flashed the red signaling lamp but there was no reply.

He was seriously worried. The sudden sharp intake of breath, almost like an outcry, that he had heard, oppressed him with a sense of apprehension. What could have happened? Turning to Tom he called for full speed ahead for the trip back.

Tom was not slow in responding. He speeded the motors up to their top capacity. In the air there were no speed laws to look out for, or other motorists or pedestrians to avoid. It was a clear road. The steel stays and stanchions of the stanch Wonder ship fairly hummed as she shot forward, while an indefinable fear clutched at Jack's heart.

He knew that his father was subject to fainting spells and he had been overworking recently. Fast as the Wondership was cutting through the air it felt like an eternity to Jack before the gray walls and the well-laid-out grounds of High Towers came into view.

The boys lost no time in landing, and not waiting to place the Wondership in her shed, set out to look for Mr. Chadwick. Jupe came shuffling by on his way from the cornpatch.

"Where's dad, Jupe?" asked Jack.

"In his labveroratory, ah reckons," answered the old colored man. "Leastways ah ain't obfustucated any obserwations ob him round der contagiois atmosferics."

"Come on, Tom," said Jack. "Let's get to dad's workshop as quick as we can."

"Why, Jack, you—you don't think that anything has happened to him, do you?" asked Tom.

"I don't know. He was talking quite cheerfully to me and then, without any warning, he gave a sort of gasp and then everything was silent."

The next minute the boys entered the workshop of the inventor.

Jack's worst fears were realized as they gazed at the scene before them. On the floor, stretched out inanimate before the radio telephone apparatus, lay Mr. Chadwick. His right hand grasped a letter.

His head lay in a pool of blood, oozing from a cut at the back of his head.

"Dad! dad! What has happened?" cried Jack, in an agony of alarm, as he fell to his knees at his father's side.

But Mr. Chadwick did not answer. The next moment Tom's shout for help brought everybody about the place running toward the workshop where the alarming discovery had been made.

CHAPTER XVIII

INTO THE STORM

"Carry him into the house and get him to bed," cried Mrs. Bagley, the housekeeper, wringing her hands distractedly. "Oh dear! poor gentleman, he's bin a-workin' too hard, that's what's the matter."

Jupe and Hank Hawkins, the handy man, picked the unconscious man up and carried him to bed, where he was made comfortable.

Jack and Tom made an investigation of the workshop. At first the cut on Mr. Chadwick's head had given Jack the impression that he might have been the victim of foul play.

But a brief survey of the place soon dispelled these conclusions. When he fell, the inventor struck his head against the sharp corner of a table right behind him, Jack concluded, and in this way inflicted the wound.

The letter that his father had been reading when he was stricken still lay on the floor. Jack picked it up. It was from the brokers in New York, the same missive Mr. Chadwick had referred to over the radio 'phone just before the silence that so alarmed Jack.

Glancing over it Jack's eyes widened. He perceived at once that the cause of his father's sudden attack no doubt lay in the shock he had received when he opened the envelope. The letter was curt and to the point.

"Your securities wiped out in panic," it said. "Wire us and advise what to do."

That was all, but it was enough. Jack knew that most of his father's money was invested with the firm that had written the letter, and now they had been wiped out in a money panic. Jack had no idea how much of his father's fortune was affected, but it was evident from Mr. Chadwick's collapse that he had been dealt a heavy blow.

He was in the midst of talking to Tom about the letter when the housekeeper came running from the house.

"Oh, here you boys are!" she exclaimed. "You must get Dr. Mays at once. Those red drops he gave your father are finished and I can't find any more."

"I'll telephone," said Jack promptly, stuffing the letter into his pocket.

"I've already tried that," said Mrs. Bagley, "but the line is out of order."

"Can't we get some other doctor?" asked Tom.

Mrs. Bagley shook her head.

"Dr. Mays is the only one who understands your father's case," she said. "You must get him as soon as possible."

"Is dad conscious yet?" asked Jack anxiously.

"Yes, he has been trying to tell me something but I won't let him talk."

"We'll get Dr. Mays right away," said Jack, but then he

suddenly recollected that the electric car was slightly out of order. There would be no time to stop and repair it then.

Luckily the Wondership still stood outside the shed. Five minutes later the boys were soaring aloft, bound for the doctor's house, which was some distance away. It was not till they had fairly started that they noticed the change in the weather.

The thunderheads they had seen earlier in the day now spread and covered the whole sky with a dark pall. The air was very still, as if nature was holding her breath. Far off, though in plain view, the sea was lying like a smooth sheet of steel-gray velvet. A sailing ship, with sails flapping, was becalmed some distance from shore.

"Going to rain," said Tom.

"Worse than that, I think," said Jack. "We're in for the storm that's been making up for two days now."

"Well, we can get there and back before it breaks."

"Easily. Let those motors out, Tom, we want to make good time."

It was oppressively hot, and had it not been for Jack's anxiety he would have enjoyed the swift cooling passage through the thundery air. But he was strangely troubled. Did that letter mean that his father was on the verge of ruin?

Suddenly he bethought himself of Ned Nevins' letter. He opened it, having pushed it into his pocket when they entered the workshop, where Mr. Chadwick had placed it before opening the ominous epistle from his brokers. It was a friendly, chatty note from the boy, and enclosed the checks covering the joint dividends of Jack and Tom in the Hydroaeroplane Company.

"Well, at any rate, that's something," declared Jack to Tom, as he handed him the letter and his check.

"Yes, but if Uncle Chester is ruined, it's only a drop in the bucket," said Tom.

"Well, it's no use crossing your bridges till you come to them," said Jack, "and anyhow, that letter may be only a false alarm. I've heard they get these financial panics in Wall Street just like kids get the measles, and they get over them as quickly."

"I trust it will be so in this case," said Tom.

"So do I," said Jack hopefully, but a cold fear that his father was ruined possessed him, and made his heart feel heavy as lead.

Suddenly, from the purple firmament, came the sound of distant thunder. Following it a puff of wind, hot as the exhalation of an opened oven, blew in their faces. In the distance they saw a ragged streak of lightning tear the cloud curtains.

CHAPTER XIX

THE "LIGHTNING CAGE"

"Look at that, will you!" exclaimed Tom.

"What, you are not scared, are you?" asked Jack.

"N-no, but I must say I'm not fond of thunderstorms Particularly when we are carrying all that gas over our heads."

"That new invention of mine will take care of that all right," said Jack confidently.

He referred to a new device of his with which the Wondership was equipped for protecting balloon bags from lightning. In a thunderstorm a balloon, or gas-filled dirigible, is subject to sudden variations of electric charge which, under certain conditions, might produce sparks leading to its annihilation.

More especially was this the case with such a craft as this Wondership, carrying as she did so much metal and steel wiring. The netting of the bag, with the idea of making it as conductive as possible, was of metal, connecting with the other metal parts of the craft so that when a steel drag rope was lowered to the ground a discharge of lightning striking the balloon would be passed off harmlessly into the earth, as is the case with a lightning conductor.

It might be supposed that making the outside of a balloon a

good conductor would invite danger from lightning. But the Boy Inventors knew that this was not the case. While the ordinary balloon envelope is a fairly good insulator against low voltage, it is unable to resist the high tension of atmospheric electricity.

Jack ascertained these facts by touching an electroscope with a bit of balloon cloth of the kind used on the Wondership, and charged with 2,000 volts of electricity. The electroscope instantly responded.

This showed that the balloon bag increased the electrical tension immediately above and below it as much as it would do if it was a perfect conductor, but the destructive action of a lightning bolt would be greater in proportion to the resistance opposed to it. So that, in reality, Jack's device was one of the safest that could be imagined for protecting balloonists in a heavy storm.

In effect, the occupants of the Wondership were enclosed in a cage. Lightning might zip through the wires and stays, but it could not touch them. As to the danger of letting out gas through the valve in a strong electric field, which is almost certain to produce sparks, the boys did not have to worry about that for to deflate the bag they simply pumped some of its contents back into the reservoir with the powerful gas pumps.

But after all, Jack's device had never been tested. It looked as if it was due to be. The wind came in sharp puffs, now hot and now cold.

Ragged, white clouds, like wind-driven fragments of filmy lace, began to whip across the dark heavens. The sea turned a peculiar light green and was flecked with whitecaps.

"We're in for it," said Jack. "Better get up the storm curtains, Tom."

While Jack steered, Tom drew up the waterproof curtains and top which, in rainy weather, made the Wondership quite dry and weather-tight. Mica portholes gave light inside this extemporized cabin, and enabled the steersman to see.

This had hardly been done when a wild gust of wind struck the Wondership and sent it staggering off its course. But in a jiffy Jack regained control of the craft and headed her straight for the white house occupied by Dr. Mays, which could now be seen, its lofty cupola poking up above the trees surrounding it.

"Glad we're nearly there," said Tom. "I don't much like this."

"We're O.K.," Jack assured him. "We went through a lot worse than this in that circular storm in Yucatan."

"Can't we drop and run along the road?"

"It's much longer by the road than by the air line, and remember we are in a big hurry."

"That's so. But we've got the return trip ahead of us."

"Well, if it gets too bad, we'll have to come back by road," said Jack, "but I haven't got a doubt that she'll stand anything that will come out of this storm."

Crash!

The sky was rent from end to end by jagged lightning. With a deafening roar the thunder broke, rumbling and crashing in the sultry air.

S-w-i-s-h!

The rain came in torrents, tearing at the storm curtains. It beat frantically at them with a noise like that of surf on a beach. But inside the boys were snug and dry, and the Wondership forged steadily forward. It was a weird experience for the boys. About them the artillery of heaven thundered and flashed. They could see each other's faces and the black outlines of their craft in the livid flare of flash after flash of lightning.

Jack, with his hands firmly gripping the steering wheel, anticipating every move of the storm-tossed Wondership like a skillful pilot, felt his pulses throb. There was something fine in battling with the elements like this in a stanch craft they had perfected. He felt that no other airship then in existence would have been able to keep up the fight.

All at once there came a crash that drove his eardrums in. The Wondership staggered and then seemed to leap into lambent flame. Blinded, Jack threw his hands before his eyes, utterly forgetting for the minute the steering wheel.

Tom gave a shout of alarm, as he felt the craft stagger as if dealt a mortal blow, and then begin to drop earthward.

"We've been struck!" he yelled in panic.

CHAPTER XX

THROUGH THE AIR

For the fraction of a second the faculties of both boys were paralyzed. A tingling sensation was in their limbs. Jack was the first to recover his wits. He snatched his hands from his eyes and seized the wheel. In a jiffy the Wondership's earthward plunge was checked. Once more she regained an even keel.

"Wh-what happened?" stuttered Tom anxiously.

"We were hit by lightning," replied Jack.

"Goodness! I thought we were goners, for a minute."

"I confess that I did, too. But I guess the 'electric cage' worked. Everything seems to be shipshape."

Jack was right. Thanks to his ingenious invention, the lightning, which had struck the aircraft, had been diffused through the safety "cage" and safely convoyed to the earth by the ground chain made of light manganese bronze, which had been lowered when the storm broke.

"Just the same I don't want to get hit again," said Tom. "I thought for a minute the world had come to an end."

"My fingers are tingling yet," said Jack, "and I can see stars, but I think if it hadn't been for the cage we would have likely been blown to smithereens."

By this time they were almost over the doctor's house and extensive grounds. Jack manipulated the Wondership against the storm, flying in a circle, and snapped on the powerful searchlight. With the help of its rays he picked out a good landing place, and having set the pumps at work abstracting gas from the bag, they soon made a good landing.

Doctor Mays stood on his porch as they left the ship and ran through the downpour for the house.

"Gracious, boys!" he exclaimed, "but you certainly gave me a fright. I thought when that bolt hit you that you were going to be annihilated."

"How did it look from below?" asked Jack.

"As if you were enveloped in blue flame. Then suddenly a ball of red fire slid from the ship to the ground—"

"Down the conducting rope," put in Jack.

"And exploded with a loud bang when it struck the ground," continued the doctor. "But all's well that ends well, and now tell me what brings you here, for I know it must be urgent business or you'd never have ventured through such a storm."

Jack hastily told the doctor of his father's stroke. The medical man looked grave.

"I'll go with you just as soon as I can pack my bag," he said. "Your father had been overworking. I warned him of what would happen if he did not rest up, some time ago, but he has, seemingly, disregarded my advice."

In a few minutes the doctor, muffled up in a raincoat, was ready to start. But he stipulated that the run to High Towers should be made by the road.

"I like excitement as well as anybody," he said, "and I've been up in your Wondership before—"

"When it was the Roadracer," interpolated Jack.

"Exactly; but I must confess that when I saw you a short time ago looking like a floating ball of fire, I lost my taste for aerial travel."

"We'll go back by road, then," said Jack, as through the rain, which was falling in torrents, they ran to the Wondership.

"My, but you have it snug in here," said the doctor, as he entered the tight, waterproof cabin.

"Hang up your coat, doctor," said Tom, and he took the physician's dripping mackintosh and slung it on a hook attached to one of the stanchions. Then the start was made, with the bag partially deflated and lying in limp, wet folds on its framework.

Through the night, under skies fretted with lightning, the Wondership shot forward. Out on the open road Jack ordered full speed, the great searchlights illuming the roadway as if it were day. He felt little apprehension of meeting other vehicles. The night was too bad to permit of any save emergency traveling.

The roads were deep in mud, and water spurted up from the wheels of the flying car as it raced through the storm. But seated snug and dry in the cabin none of them bothered about this. Little was said. Jack had to concentrate his mind on handling the Wondership, for driving under the conditions, and at such speed, required all the wheel-handler's attention.

On and on they flew, down hills and over bridges, under which, ordinarily, quiet streams flowed, but now swollen by the rains, they boiled and raced like angry torrents. They flashed through villages and past farmhouses without encountering a soul, while overhead the tempest roared and raged and flared.

They were shooting down a hill at top speed when Jack suddenly gave a gasp. Right in front of them, vividly outlined in the searchlight's glare, was an obstacle. A big wagonload of hay, covered with a tarpaulin, and deserted by its driver who, despairing of mounting the hill in the storm, had unhitched his horses and driven off till the weather cleared.

The wagon was in such a position that it blocked the road, which was sunken between high banks at that point. Jack ground down his brakes in chagrin.

"Blocked!" he exclaimed disgustedly.

CHAPTER XXI

VAULTING TO THE RESCUE

"What awful luck," muttered Tom.

"Isn't there any way we can get by?" inquired the doctor anxiously. "It's important that I should reach Mr. Chadwick as soon as possible."

Jack made no reply, but bent over the gas-valve. In an instant the gas was hissing into the balloon bag. Its wet folds swelled out, and presently Jack started the propellers. Like a racehorse leaping a barrier, the Wondership rose skyward.

"Hold fast!" cried the boy in a triumphant voice.

"Wow!" yelled Tom, "there are more ways of killing a cat than by choking it with cream."

The next moment the Wondership was in the road on the other side of the hay wagon, having hurdled it like a high jumper, and was once more on her way.

"Jove, you boys are marvels!" exclaimed the doctor. "Is there anything you can't do with this craft, or auto, or whatever it is, of yours?"

"Lots of things, I guess," said Tom, "but we haven't found many of them yet."

At uninterrupted speed the journey was resumed. At times so swift was the pace that the Wondership seemed to be half flying. Thanks to her shock absorbers, but little motion was felt, although in places the roadway had been washed out by the torrential downpour and was very rough.

"Whereabouts are we?" shouted Tom, as they rushed along.

"Near the Coon Creek Bridge," flung back Jack over his shoulder. "We ought to sight it at any moment now."

He peered through the blackness ahead. The searchlights failed to show any bridge. But the young driver saw an abandoned cottage by the roadside which had formerly been used as a toolhouse. Just beyond it he knew the bridge should loom up with its white railings.

But there was not a sign of it.

Not till it was too late to stop did Jack realize what had happened. The bridge had been washed away by the rising waters of the creek and he was tearing at top speed for the steep banks.

It was a moment for lightning thinking. Right ahead loomed a black pit which he knew marked the water course.

Suddenly it flashed into Jack's mind that in former times, before the bridge had been built, there had been a ford at the point.

The banks, steep elsewhere, almost wall-like in fact, were still graded at the place where the old crossing spot had been.

He jerked over the steering wheel with a suddenness that threatened to overturn the Wondership. The auto-craft plunged wildly to one side and then rushed downward.

Before he realized it, Jack had steered her into the rushing waters of the swollen creek.

"All the power you've got," he cried to Tom, as the Wondership careened and tipped madly and then recovered an even keel. Jack headed her up stream while Tom, who hardly knew what had happened, blindly obeyed orders.

Jack's chief fear was that the rush of the torrential water would carry him too far down to make a landing on the opposite side of the old ford. In that case they would be in a bad fix, for the creek ran for some distance between steep walls of limestone rock.

It was a hard struggle. The twin propellers beat the air furiously, clawing the Wondership up stream, while the water hissed and roared all about her, and the engine labored with a noise like that of a giant locust.

And then, almost before he knew it, and before either Tom or the doctor realized in the least what had happened, they found themselves safe on the other side. They had gained the opposite slope of the ford with hardly an inch to spare, but that was enough.

The Wondership sped up the bank as if glad to be free of the battle with the swollen creek, and not half an hour afterward they rolled up to High Towers.

Dr. Mays was met almost tearfully by Mrs. Bagley.

"How is he?" was his first question.

"He seems to be better, doctor, but something is worrying him," said the worthy woman.

"I'll go up to him at once. You boys had better stay here," said the doctor.

The physician was upstairs a long time. When he came down

he looked grave.

"Is dad any better?" asked Jack anxiously.

"He is suffering from a nervous breakdown due to overwork," said the doctor. "The cut on his head is a mere flesh wound. But he appears to have something on his mind. Do you know what it is?"

Then, and not till then, for in the rush of events he had completely forgotten it, Jack remembered the letter from the brokers.

"Dr. Mays," he said, "you are an old friend?"

"I hope so, my boy. You may confide in me freely if you know any reason for your father's disquiet."

"If you will read this, doctor, you will understand," and Jack handed him the letter.

Dr. Mays read it with knitted brows.

"So this explains it," he said as he returned it to Jack. "Your father kept muttering about foolish speculations and ruin, but would not tell me what he meant. Now it is all clear. Poor Chadwick, I'm afraid from what he said that his fortune, all but a small amount, is wiped out."

"But will he get better, doctor?" asked Jack anxiously, disregarding the monetary aspect of the affair.

"That all depends," said the doctor seriously, "on his freedom from anxiety."

"You mean that he must not worry over money matters?"

"Precisely; but, as that letter states he is ruined, it will be hard to set his mind at rest. If there were only some way of meeting the situation!"

In the crucible of that moment an idea was borne to Jack that was destined to lead him into strange paths.

"I think I know of a way," he said quietly, "that is, if the brokers' message is not exaggerated."

But it was not. The next day confirmatory reports arrived of the wreck of Mr. Chadwick's fortunes. In his room, attended constantly by Dr. Mays, his friend as well as physician, the inventor raved of his losses.

"We have got to think of some way of easing his mind," said Dr. Mays, who had placed his regular practice in the hands of another doctor so that he might be with Mr. Chadwick. "If only his fortune could be won back."

"I think I know of a way," said Jack quietly.

The doctor stared at him as if he thought the boy had taken leave of his senses.

"You know of a way?" he questioned incredulously.

"Yes, sir. At least if the information Tom and I have on the subject is correct."

"I don't follow you," said the puzzled doctor. "Your father has lost thousands."

Jack nodded.

"I know all that," he said.

"And yet you are prepared to get it back?"

"I said I thought there was a possibility," was Jack's quiet reply.

"And what may that be?"

"Did you ever hear of Z.2.X., doctor?" was the entirely unexpected question.

CHAPTER XXII

"Z.2.X"

"Z.2.X.? Well, such things are rather out of my line, but I have heard of it—yes," replied the doctor, looking more puzzled than ever. "But what do you know about it?"

"Till two days ago—nothing," replied Jack, "but now I believe that I know where there is a trainload of it."

"Good heavens, boy, you don't know what you're talking about. Why, the stuff is as valuable—as valuable as radium. Possibly it is worth more."

"Then even a small quantity would restore my father's fortune and his health?" asked Jack, persisting in his line of inquiry.

"Undoubtedly it would restore his fortune, and in my belief his health, which he is unlikely to gain otherwise."

"Then I'll do it," said Jack, speaking for himself and Tom, for the two lads had discussed the idea the night before. "Those dividends from our share of the hydroaeroplane plant will fit out an expedition, and if we fail—well, we can still sell out our interest and help dad get on his feet again."

The telephone bell jangled. Jack answered it. The voice that came over the wire was that of Professor Jenks. His tones trembled with excitement as he spoke to the boy.

"I have analyzed that sample from the Colorado River," he said.

"Well, what is your verdict?" asked Jack, with a painfully beating heart.

"That when all the expenses of reduction and refining and transportation and digging are deducted that it will be worth at least $100 an ounce," was the reply. "It would bring an even higher price, for the placing of a large amount on the market will probably have the effect of lowering it."

"Great Scott!" breathed Jack, "and there's a whole island of it there for the taking."

"Yes; but how are yow going to get it? The cliffs are unscalable, the river unnavigable. It might as well be in Mars for all the good it does anyone," objected the professor.

Jack's next words were direct, to say the least.

"I've figured out all that," he said. "We can get it, if it's there to be got. I've a reason now for going out there if it's possible to come to some arrangement with Zeb Cummings. Can you meet me at the hospital this afternoon to talk over the matter?"

"Are you serious?" gasped the professor.

"Perfectly," Jack assured him. "If we can't get at it by earth or water we can reach it from the air, can't we?"

"Heaven bless my soul, I never thought of that," choked out the professor. "I—Melissa's calling me. I'll meet you at the hospital this afternoon."

"Tom and I will be there," said Jack, but the professor, at the imperious bidding of Melissa, had hung up the receiver.

The result of the conference held that afternoon at the bedside of Zeb Cummings was the formation of the Z.2.X. Exploration Company, the members being Jack, Tom, Zeb Cummings and the professor. The capital was to be furnished in equal amounts by the professor and the boys, and Zeb Cummings was to be an equal partner in the enterprise, he having furnished the information on which Jack hoped to rehabilitate his father's fortunes.

As for the professor, he did not so much regard the pecuniary side of the expedition as the opportunity he would have to write an epoch-making book and confound his scientific rivals. In their enthusiasm, the adventurers did not take into consideration the fact that the map might be wrong, or that the strange metals be just visionary deposits. The boys' enthusiasm drowned all doubts in their minds; Zeb and the professor never were as optimistic.

Dr. Mays, when he had been placed in full possession of the facts and considered them, decided that under the circumstances the boys could go and undertook to quiet any apprehensions Mr. Chadwick might have concerning the trip. It was found that enough had been saved from the wreck of the inventor's fortunes to enable him to live comfortably while the boys were away, besides which he had royalties from several inventions coming in. Still, the bulk of his fortunes had vanished and the radio telephone was not yet a practicable instrument to put upon the market.

But with Z.2.X. the boys hoped to make it a perfect transmitter of speech over great distances.

Of course, Jack's plan was to utilize the Wondership on the enterprise of finding Rattlesnake Island and its treasures. After long consultations with Zeb, who was now convalescent, it was decided to ship the craft, in sections, to Yuma on the Colorado River and make the start secretly from some point below there.

It was in the midst of these plans, and while the boys' workshed was littered with lists of provisions and equipment that Dick Donovan injected himself into the situation. The red-headed young reporter descended upon them one day when they were busily packing the Wondership away in big crates, which were labeled in various ways so as to give no inkling of the contents.

Of course Dick, being in a way a member of the firm, had to be told what was going on, and the result was that after a lot of hard pleading the boys consented to allow him to come along.

"He's got red hair," said Zeb, "and that ought to make him good on the trail, same as a buckskin cayuse."

The boys didn't quite see the logic of this, but they knew from former experiences that the young reporter was a good campmate, and they were, on the whole, glad that they had included him. But when young Donovan came to High Towers, he was not aware that he was followed by Bill Masterson, who, as we know, was the son of the proprietor of the *Boston Moon*, on which paper young Masterson also worked as a reporter.

Ever since Dick Donovan had written for his paper, the *Boston Evening Eagle*, the wonderful story of the boys' adventures on the trail of the giant sloth of Brazil, other Boston reporters had regarded him as worth watching. In some way, young Masterson learned of Dick's frequent visits to High Towers while the preparations for the Colorado trip were going forward.

"It's my idea," he told his father, "that those Boy Inventors are planning another big stunt and that Dick Donovan is to go along and write the story. Do we want to get beaten again?"

"We do not," said his father, a heavily-set, dictatorial man, perpetually at war with the *Evening Eagle*. "That last beat of Donovan's on the Brazil story jumped the *Eagle's* circulation sky high."

"Well, why not let me trail along after them and find out what I can?" said young Masterson. "No use letting the *Moon* get soaked again, and besides, I want to get even on those young fellows, anyhow, for the mean trick they played in having me arrested, even if it didn't come to anything, and the case was dropped."

"Jove!" he cried suddenly, as a new train of thought was suggested to him. "I'll bet I've got it. This trip, or whatever it is, they are planning has something to do with that miner, Zeb Cummings, the chap I ran down."

"Well, it's worth keeping a weather eye on, anyway," decided his father. "I guess you'll get the assignment."

"And I'll run it down, too," declared young Masterson boastfully. "I owe that red-headed, chesty Donovan a grudge anyhow."

That evening young Masterson met by appointment the two youths who had been with him in the automobile the day that Zeb was run down. They were both sons of wealthy men, and had more money than was good for them. Masterson found that both Sam Higgins and Eph Compton were willing to do all they could to harm the boys who had been responsible for their arrests, and so it came about that Jupe, on his way to the village to post some letters, was enticed into talk one night, and while he was chatting and accepting the good cigars three amiable young men pressed upon him, the mail was abstracted from his pocket.

There were two letters, one from Dick to his city editor telling him of the progress made and informing him of the day for the start, and the other from Jack to his father, who was a guest of Dr. Mays. Jack gave full details of their plans and other information concerning the trip, so that the three plotters, a few days before the expedition set out, knew as much about it as the boys themselves.

Armed with this information, Masterson, Higgins and Compton had no difficulty in getting money from their parents, all of whom would have described themselves as "keen business men." As for Jupe, he was too badly scared to say anything about the loss of the letters, and as Masterson, after steaming them open and abstracting what he wanted of their contents, posted them to their proper destinations, the boys started out on their long journey west without the slightest idea that anyone but themselves and one or two others knew of their plans.

The professor's going was not unaccompanied by difficulties. Miss Melissa had insisted that if he was to accompany the expedition, she was going along, too. This being manifestly impossible, the man of science was driven to the subterfuge of placing a bag of fossils in his bed to represent him. On the night of the start, Miss Melissa looked into his room every few minutes to make sure he had not escaped.

It was not till morning that she discovered that the man of science had effected his escape through his bedroom window, climbing down a latticework to the ground. At first she was half inclined to pursue him, but thought the better of it when she read the note the professor had left behind.

"Well," said Miss Melissa to her little maid, "there's one good thing—he won't be cluttering up the house with old stones and rocks for some time to come."

"What shall I do with them fossils what he put in his bed to make believe it was him, miss?" asked the maid.

"You may throw them into the creek at the back of the house, Mary," said Miss Melissa, and went placidly about her dusting and sweeping and "setting to rights."

But of all this, the professor, on the train speeding westward, was blissfully unconscious. Perhaps even if he had known it, he would not have cared much, for even his scientific mind was warmed and thrilled by the prospect of the aerial search for the mineral treasures of Rattlesnake Island.

CHAPTER XXIII

ON THE BORDER LINE

The long train of gray-coated coaches, filmed with the arid dust of the desert, rolled into Yuma, the little town at the junction of the Gila and Colorado River, popularly supposed to be the hottest place in America. The boys, glad that their long journey had come to an end, felt that it was living up to its reputation as they alighted and stood in the blistering heat while their personal baggage was thrown off.

The professor, however, was quite oblivious to the scorching rays of the afternoon sun. He darted about seeking specimens, and he had soon gathered up quite a collection of small rocks. In the meantime Zeb Cummings, who was quite in his element, had helped the boys get their things together and see them loaded on a mule wagon which rattled them off to a small hotel, for they did not want to make themselves any more conspicuous than was necessary.

The boys wore gray flannel shirts, khaki trousers, stout high boots and broad-brimmed hats, and had fastened red handkerchiefs round their throats to keep off the sun from the back of their necks. Zeb had a similar outfit.

The professor, however, still wore his baggy black garments, his only concession to the heat being a big green umbrella, which looked like a gigantic verdant mushroom. As they drove off in a rickety sort of bus, having with difficulty persuaded the professor to leave off specimen hunting for a while, the boys did not notice that from the opposite side of the train three young men had alighted who, from a point of vantage behind a water tower, watched their movements.

The trio were Bill Masterson and his two cronies, Sam Higgins and Eph Compton.

"Well, here we are, Eph," said Bill, as they watched the boys drive off.

"Yes, and here they are, too," grunted Eph.

"I'm glad we've got here at last, though. Keeping out of sight on that train was beginning to get on my nerves."

"Same here," said Sam Higgins, stretching himself. "But I guess we succeeded in keeping ourselves hidden all right."

"Sure," rejoined Masterson. "They haven't a notion we are here."

In the meantime the lads found accommodations till the next day at the small hotel on a back street where Zeb had insisted on their coming so as to escape observation. Yuma is full of prospectors and miners, and every stranger in town is suspected of having some sort of a scheme, he explained, and as a consequence is closely watched.

Zeb's first care, therefore, was to circulate a story that the professor, a noted savant and geologist, was going into the desert with his party to collect specimens. This appeared to satisfy the landlord, who was at first inclined to be curious.

The professor had hardly been shown his room before he was out again with his hammer and satchel and his attention was almost at once attracted by a big stone that held up one corner of the barn at the back of the hotel. The boys knew nothing of what he was doing till they heard a loud, angry voice crying:

"Hey, you in ther preacher's suit! Quit tryin' ter pull thet thar barn down, will yer?"

"But, my dear sir," came the professor's voice, in mild expostulation, "are you aware that you have built your barn on the top of a splendid specimen of primordial rock?"

"Don't know nuthin' about a prime order of rock," came back the other voice.

The boys looked out of the window. They saw the landlord of the hotel, a surly-looking fellow, with a big black mustache and tanned cheeks, striding across the yard to the professor, who had blissfully resumed his chipping.

The landlord reached out one brawny hand to grab his guest, when something happened that made him temporarily cease hostilities. A big chunk of rock suddenly flaked off under the professor's assault. It flew in the air and the next instant a yell of pain apprised them that the landlord had got it right in the eye.

The professor looked round as the man emitted a bellow of rage.

"Bless me, where did that bit of rock go? Ah, there it is! Right at your feet, sir," and he darted forward with a smile of satisfaction and, picking up the chunk of rock that had struck the indignant landlord, placed it in his satchel.

"Thank you very much for stopping it, sir," he said, with a bow, and then, before the thunderstruck landlord could say anything, the scientist strolled off under his umbrella in search of more specimens. The boys fairly choked with laughter.

But the landlord was too dumfounded even to speak for a minute. His face grew as purple as a plum. He appeared to be about to burst.

"He's locoed," he burst forth at last, "locoed as a horn toad, by the 'tarnal hills."

Then, holding a hand to his eye, he reentered the hotel and could be heard shouting for hot water to bathe his injury.

Zeb, who had been out looking for a trustworthy man to take their effects out to a spot along the river where they could put the Wondership together without exciting undue curiosity, returned shortly before supper with news that he had been successful in his search, an old, wrinkled prospector named Pete McGee, who had learned the secret of silence during the long years he had spent on the desert.

After the evening meal old McGee put in an appearance and a bargain was struck. But if he was, as Zeb put it, "close-mouthed" on some subjects, he was not on others.

"So yer are a'goin' out inter the desert, hey?" he asked the boys.

"That's our intention," said Dick.

The old man shook his head.

"The desert's a tough place," he said. "A mighty tough place. Reckon it's likely yer are er goin' prospectin', maybe?"

The boys returned an evasive answer. But old McGee rambled on with the crisscross wrinkles forming and fading round his washed-out blue eyes.

"Wa'al, I had my share on it, ain't I, Zeb?" said the old man to Zeb, who had just strolled up, smoking a short, black pipe. The professor, after adjusting his difficulties with the landlord, was sorting and labeling specimens in his room.

"Reckon you have, Pete," responded the yellow-bearded miner. "You didn't never find that thar lost Peg-leg Smith mine, did yer?"

"No; but I will some day," declared the old man, a fanatic gleam shining in his faded optics. "I'll find it some day, Zeb. I never got to it, but I come mighty close—yes, sir, ole Pete he come mighty close."

"Tell the boys about Peg-leg Smith's lost mine," suggested Zeb.

"Give me the fillin's, then, an' I will," said old Pete, holding out a blackened and empty corncob, "though I'm surprised they ain't never heard on it. Thought everybody had heard of Peg-leg's mine."

"Wa'al, you see they come frum ther East," explained Zeb apologetically.

"Ah, that accounts fer it," said old Pete indulgently. "You couldn't 'spec Easterners ter know nuthin' 'bout it. 'Wa'al, young sirs, somewheres out on the desert ter the east uv here thar is three buttes a stickin' up, and right thar is Peg-leg Smith's lost mine whar they say the very sands is uv gold.

"Who was Peg-leg? Wa'al, that's in a way not very well known. Anyhow, his name was Smith, and he was shy an off leg, and so he gets his name. Back in 1836 Peg-leg he blows inter Yuma with a party of trappers that hed worked down ther Colorado.

"They decides to quit trapping and go ter gold huntin', and makes their way up the Gila River and then cuts off inter ther desert. Frum Yuma they goes southeast and kep' on fer four days across the desert. At ther end of the fourth day they 'lows that ther water ain' a-goin' ter hold out a turrible lot longer, and they decides to look fer a water-hole in a canyon at ther end uv which stands three lone buttes sticking up, like sentinels against ther sky.

"Wa'al, they hunts ther canyon through but nary a drop of water. In time they reaches ther buttes. They climbs to ther top ter see what might lay beyond, but they see nuthin' but ther same God-forgotten country.

"But Peg-leg, who fer all he was minus a limb, could travel with any of 'em, he finds at the top of the southernmost butte a lot of chunks of black rock lying round promiscous, an' some of them has specks an' chunks of yaller as bright as Zeb's beard on 'em. Peg-leg he opines ther yaller is nuthin' but copper, or maybe fool's gold.

"That night they camps, feelin' considerable blue, fer ther's mighty little water left an' they've come too far ter go back. But in ther distance thar's a big mountain and they make up their minds they'll find water thar or bust and wither on the desert.

"Ther next evening, more dead than alive, they reaches the mountain and finds a little spring. It was ther finest thing they'd seen fer a long time, and in honor of Peg-leg, who suggested going to ther mountain, they calls it Smith Mountain, and that's its name to this day. In time they worked round to San Bernardino and then Smith he hunts up a mineral sharp who tells him that what he had found was gold.

"Wa'al, Smith was a curious feller, frum all accounts, and it was not till '49 when ther big gold rush came that he thought much more about those three buttes with the gold lying round loose as dirt on 'em. Then he got ther gold fever. He went to 'Frisco and gets up an expedition to find them three buttes.

"They got down inter ther desert country all right and locates Smith Mountain. But the dern Indians they had with 'em as guides cleaned out the camp one fine night, and they had a hard time getting back to civilization alive. Well, that's where Peg-leg Smith goes out of the story."

"Wasn't he ever heard of again?" asked Jack.

"No, siree, not hide nor hair on him. Nobody never knows what became of him arter they got back to San Bernardino. Some says that he went back alone lookin' fer the three buttes and was lost in the desert and that his bones is out thar some'eres to-day, an' others says that he got so plum disgusted he went back home to St. Louis. But nobody rightly knows.

"The next heard of ther three buttes was many years later when an Indian, who worked on Governor Downey's ranch, not far from Smith Mountain, developed a habit of goin' away fer a few days and then comin' back with bits of black rock chock full of gold which he traded fer firewater and such. He didn't seem ter care if he got full value or not.

"Plenty more where those came from," he'd say.

"Wa'al, they set a watch on him and found that he always headed off inter ther desert by way of Smith Mountain, which would be the nat'ul way of gettin' ter ther three buttes that Peg-leg had described.

"Guv'ner Downey he come to hear about this in course of time, and he come down frum Sacramento to question ther Injun. But in ther meantime ther pesky coyote had gone and got himself killed in a quarrel over cards and so there they was up agains' a blank wall ag'in."

The old prospector paused to fill his pipe.

CHAPTER XXIV

"THE THREE BUTTES"

"The Injun bein' dead, the guv'ner did the nex' best thing. He questioned his squaw. But she couldn't tell 'em much 'cept that the Injun told her he got his last water at t'other side of Smith Mountain and then traveled toward ther sun till erbout mid-afternoon when he found mucho, mucho oro.

"The guv'ner made two or three tries to locate them buttes, but he failed. Then come along a man named McGuire, who said he knew where the buttes was and showed black rocks with gold in 'em to prove it, jes' like the ones Peg-leg and ther Injun had found, they was. Well, McGuire he gets five other dern fools and off they starts and that's the end of them. They ain't never heard of ag'in.

"Then comes a prospector who gets lost, and in hunting for water finds these same three buttes and the black, gold-specked rocks that are scattered about. But he wasn't bothering about gold just then, so he keeps on and in time finds the water hole at the foot of Smith Mountain.

"He comes back to Los Angeles and tries to organize a company to go to ther three buttes. But he falls ill and when he learns he's goin' ter die he tells Dr. De Courcy, that's his physician, that he knows whar Peg-leg's lost mine is an' gives him a map an' directions. Arter ther man dies, Dr. De Courcy spends all his money trying ter find ther buttes, but he fails.

Then comes a young chap named Tom Cover of Riverside. He's wealthy and fits out a dozen or more outfits to hunt fer ther three buttes. But after setting out on his twelfth trip he never comes back, so they know that Peg-leg Smith's mine has claimed another victim."

"Is there anything to prove that Peg-leg really ever found the Three Buttes?" asked Tom, whom this romance of the desert, like his companions, had strangely interested.

"You tell 'em, Zeb," said the old man. "Likely they wouldn't believe me."

"Proofs?" said Zeb, "plenty of 'em. The records of the old Bank of San Francisco show that McGuire deposited thousands of dollars' worth of gold nuggets there, and my old dad knew Peg-leg Smith and saw the black rocks with the gold fillings that he brought out uv ther desert. Them three golden buttes is out thar somewhar's, and some day somebody's goin' to locate 'em and then there'll be another millionaire in the country."

Old McGee chuckled over his pipe. It was clear that, ancient and feeble as he was, he still believed with all the fanaticism and optimism of a prospector that he would be the one to find the three buttes of gold.

"It stands ter reason thar's gold out thar," declared old man McGee, waving his pipe about argumentatively. "Ther good Lord never made nuthin' thet wasn't of some use, even ther fleas on a houn' dawg, for they keep him frum thinkin' uv his troubles. Very well, then, the desert is good fer nuthin' else but mineral wealth, and Providence made it so plagued hard ter git at so that everyone couldn't git rich at oncet."

The boys had to laugh at this bit of philosophy, but as they went to bed they could not help thinking of the toll of lives the great barren stretches of the Colorado desert has exacted from gold-seekers. In Jack's dreams he seemed to be traversing vast solitudes of sand and desolation dotted with bleaching bones, and he woke with a start to find that it was daybreak and that Tom was shaking him out of his sleep.

Below, old man McGee was ready with his team and had already got on his wagon some of the crates from the freight shed. They made a hasty breakfast and then started out. There was hardly anybody about and they congratulated Zeb on his strategy in conducting affairs with such secrecy.

But as they passed into the outskirts of the town, where the Mexicans and Indians lived, Dick Donovan uttered a sudden exclamation.

"Hopping horn-toads!" he gasped.

"What's up?" asked Jack, who sat beside him.

"Oh, nothing," said Dick, "the wagon gave an extra hard jolt, that was all, and I thought my head was coming off."

But the cause of Dick's exclamation had been this: From behind a squalid hut he caught sight of three shadowy figures, dimly seen in the half light, apparently watching the wagon and its occupants.

They quickly withdrew as they saw Dick looking at them, but not before the young reporter had received a startling impression that one of them at least was familiar to him. The wagon drove out over the desert and rumbled along till it came to a deep arroyo, or gulch, in which stood a deserted, bleaching hut.

"This is the place," said Zeb.

"Sure, you can stay thar fer a year an' a day an' nuthin' but tarant'las an' rattlers ull ever bother ye," said old McGee cheerfully.

The cases they had brought were quickly unloaded and lowered into the arroyo which led down to where they could see the turgid flood of the Colorado flowing between low banks. For at this spot the river is a very different stream from what it is above and below, where it makes its way to the Gulf of California between unscalable walls of cliffs and is a succession of cruel rapids and unpassable falls.

When old McGee drove back for the second and last load, for the Wondership was constructed so as to "take-down" very compactly, Dick elected to go with him. When they arrived at the freight depot the young reporter took the first opportunity to wire his paper in Boston.

"Find out if Bill Masterson is in town," was the substance of his message.

They were not to return to the camp till after the mid-day meal, so he had plenty of time to receive an answer. This is it:

"Masterson and two others left for the West five days ago."

* * * * *

"The same day that we did," mused Dick. "I wonder—but no, I'm sure. One of those three figures lurking behind that hut was Masterson, and he's planning some mischief, sure as a gun."

CHAPTER XXV

INTO THE BEYOND

"Well, this is something like camping," said Tom that evening, stretching himself out luxuriously under a mesquite bush.

"See here, young feller," said Zeb, who by unanimous consent had been put in charge of the adventurers. "Are you on a pleasure trip, jes' dropped in as a visitor like, or air you a part of this expedition?"

"I guess I'm a part of it all right," said Tom, with rather a sheepish grin. "At least I was under that impression."

"Same here," said Zeb dryly. "Thar's lots to be done yet afore we're all shipshape fer ther night. Ther's lamps ter be filled and tent ropes set right an' then I want a trench dug around ther tents."

"What's the trench for?" asked Jack, who had been busy with the three tents, for they had decided on Zeb's advice not to use the old roofless shack to sleep in.

"No tellin' what kind of varmints, from skunks to rattlers, ain't makin' a hotel out of it," he said, "not to mention tarant'las, which has a most unpleasant bite, and scorpions and centipedes that ain't much nicer bedfellows."

This was quite enough to make the boys willing, nay anxious, to set up the waterproof silk tents.

"What's the trench for?" asked Zeb. "Well, if it should come on ter rain in ther night it'll keep us dry to have a trench round each tent."

"Rain!" exclaimed Tom incredulously. "Why, it doesn't look as if it ever rained here."

"It doesn't, not more'n about two inches a year," rejoined Zeb, "but when it does you'd think ther flood gates uv heaven had been ripped wide open."

"Do you think it will rain to-night?" asked Jack.

"It looks uncommon like it," answered Zeb. "See them clouds off there yonder?"

He pointed to some heavy-looking masses of vapor hanging above a dim range of saw-backed mountains off to the east.

"In my opinion they're plum full of rain," he said.

"In that case we'd better get ready with the trenches," declared Jack. He picked up one shovel and gave another to Tom. The latter made a wry face but said nothing. Tom liked hard work no better than most boys, but he realized that the work had to be done, and so tackled it with the best grace he could.

Secretly he wished himself to be with Dick Donovan, who had been assigned to go fishing to see if he couldn't get "something" fresh for supper. The professor, as usual, was off somewhere collecting specimens.

But the task of digging the trenches was not as arduous as it had appeared. The sand was soft and yielding, and the shovels made rapid work with it. Soon a fairly deep trench was dug round each of the temporary shelters.

By the time the lanterns had been filled, and Zeb had cut a goodly stack of mesquite wood, everything was ready to begin preparations for supper.

"We'll have a blow-out to-night," said Zeb. "Canned salmon, beans, crackers, cheese and canned fruit, but don't expect to get that right along. I've lived on beans and bacon for six months in this very neck of the woods, and thought myself lucky to get that."

"Hullo!" came a cry from the direction of the river.

"There's Dick!" exclaimed both boys, and then as the young reporter came into sight, "What luck, Dick?"

"What do you know about this?" and Dick held up a fine string of glittering fish. There were catfish, perch and two eels.

"Good; we won't go hungry," said Zeb. "Nothing better than fried eels and catfish."

He greased the frying pan with a strip of bacon rind and then skinned the scaleless catfish and eels as if he had been doing nothing else all his life. Soon the savory odors of the frying with crisp slices of bacon, and the aroma of coffee, filled the camp.

The boys were so busy setting out the tin cups and plates that it was not till Zeb beat on a tin basin with a spoon to announce that the evening meal was ready that anyone noticed that the professor was missing. Night was closing in and the sky was overcast.

The boys began to worry. They set up a loud shout.

"Pro-fess-or! Oh, pro-fess-or!"

The little gulch rang with it. But no answer came.

"Now what in the world has happened to him?" frowned Jack. "We must go and find him at once. He must have—"

The sentence was never completed. At that instant Zeb set up a shout, and a ton of earth and rocks, more or less, came hurtling down the steep bank into the camp. The stones and dirt were mingled with mesquite bushes and in the midst of the landslide was a figure that they made out to be the professor.

Luckily, the avalanche had missed the camp-fire and the supper table, and when they had extricated the professor, and brushed him off, the boys learned that he had almost missed his way, and being shortsighted, in the dark had walked right over the edge of the steepest part of the arroyo instead of by a sloping path up above.

However, nothing was injured about him but his feelings, and since his bag of specimens was intact, the man of science, after a few minutes, was able to sit down and eat with as good an appetite as any of them.

Zeb proved himself a good weather profit. About midnight it started raining, and such rain as the boys had never seen. It was not rain. It was sheets of water. Even the waterproof tents began to leak, and the fact that the trenches had been dug did not serve to keep the floors dry, for the hard, sun-baked earth did not absorb the moisture, and the downpour speedily spread half an inch or more of water over the ground.

"Turn out! turn out!" shouted Dick, who shared one of the three tents with the boys.

"What's the matter?" began Tom sleepily, and then splash! went his hand into the water.

"Gracious, has the river overflowed?" demanded Jack.

"No, but it's raining handsaws and marlin spikes," cried

Dick. "Wow! my bed's wet through."

"Same here," cried Jack ruefully. "I guess we'd better get out of this."

Outside they found the professor hopping about barefooted in the water. He had on his pajamas with a blanket thrown round his shoulders for protection against the rain. The boys, despite their discomfort, could not help laughing at the odd figure. Zeb joined them, grumbling: "We made a big mistake in camping in this arroyo.

I ought to have had better sense. It's nothing more nor less than a river. All the desert up above is draining into it."

It was true. The water was almost ankle deep. Luckily, the old shanty in which their supplies were stored was raised above the ground, and the goods were all covered with a big waterproof canvas.

"Let's camp out in the shanty till daylight," suggested Jack.

"That would be a good idea if it had a roof," commented Zeb dryly.

"Why can't we spread some of the canvas over us?" asked Tom.

This was finally done, and thus passed most of their first night on the desert. Yet none of them complained, but made the best of it. The boys knew that it is the wisest plan to meet all camping mishaps with a smiling face.

By morning the rain had ceased. The sky was clear and the sun shone brightly. Their wet bedding and garments were soon dried and then the work of unpacking the sections of the Wondership was begun, for they were anxious to have the job completed and be on their way as soon as possible.

Old McGee had told the truth when he said they would not be molested.

An old Indian jogging by on a spavined horse and wrapped in a dirty blanket was the only person they saw all day. He was looking along the arroyo for a strayed burro. He stared at them in stolid silence for a while and then rode off, shaking his head. No doubt he was at a loss to account for such strange goings on.

That evening when Dick took his line down to the river, he met with unusually good luck. He had just added a fine carp to his pile of fish when, chancing to look up, he saw a boat coming round the bend.

In the craft were three figures, one of whom he recognized instantly as Masterson. The recognition was mutual and Masterson, who had the oars, started hastily to pull away from the place. But Dick shouted to him.

"Don't let me drive you away," he cried.

Masterson shouted back something about "fresh kid" but kept pulling up the stream, and soon he was round the bend and out of sight.

"Now, I wonder what he is doing out here?" mused Dick, "and those two cronies of his. They look sort of shady to me."

He cudgeled his brains to find a reason for the presence of Masterson so far from home, but was unable to arrive at any solution till an idea suddenly struck him.

"They're out here trailing us," he muttered. "Yes, I'm sure of it. But how in the world did they ever learn our plans? I guess I'll get back to camp and put the rest on their guard, for we don't want any spies hanging about, and those fellows were out on a spying expedition or I miss my guess."

CHAPTER XXVI

THE START FOR THE UNKNOWN

But the days went by, and the Wondership stood once more assembled and ready to take the greatest flight of her career, and no further sign of the three worthies, whom Dick suspected of designs against them, appeared. Zeb went to town once or twice, using a small burro for a saddle animal. Jack heard from his father, who said that he was progressing well, but was very much worried over money matters.

"If only you can find the Z.2.X.," he wrote, "we can all be happy again."

"I will find it," Jack murmured to himself, as he concluded reading the letter, and passed it over to Tom for his perusal.

Dick helped with the Wondership and spent the rest of the time fishing and hunting. He managed to get a few rabbits, but there was no other game in the vicinity. It was too barren for deer, although it was said there were plenty of them further down the river. The young reporter, who had quite a mechanical genius of his own, constructed a rough sort of boat out of boards from the walls of the old shack, and used it on his fishing expeditions, "punting" it along with a long pole made from a willow sapling from a grove on the river bank some distance below where they were camped.

One afternoon the fancy took him to pole up the current and

round the bend below which Masterson's boat had appeared the evening Dick saw and recognized the son of the *Moon* proprietor.

He had not gone that way before and was surprised to find that, instead of the low banks that edged the river where the boys were camped, round the bend were steep, almost clifflike acclivities on both sides of the stream. In places these were honeycombed with caves, running back, apparently, some distance into the bank. Although Dick did not know it, these caves had once been the dwelling places of an extinct tribe of Indians.

The boy was surprised to see smoke coming from one of them, for he had supposed that they were uninhabited.

"Maybe there are Indians up there," thought the boy. "I guess I'll give them a look, and maybe get a good picture," for Dick invariably carried his camera with him on the chance of getting a good snapshot at something or other.

A rough path led up to the cave and it was well worn by feet which had, apparently, traversed it recently. Dick reached the entrance of the cave and peered in.

It was deserted; but to his astonishment he saw, from the way it was fitted up, that whoever lived in it were not Indians. Blankets lay on the floor, and the smoke was coming from a fire which had been used for cooking and was dying out. The utensils were not such as Indians use, being made of agate ware. Then, too, he noticed some old coats and other garments hanging on nails that had been driven into the wall.

As his eyes grew more accustomed to the light, he saw a suitcase in one corner. There were initials on it. Dick made them out to be W. M.

"'W. M.'? Who can that be?" he mused. "Whoever lives here is a white man, that is plain. But why is he a hermit? Anyhow,

I'd better be getting out of this before he comes back. I've really got no business in here at all."

At this juncture he heard voices coming from the river. They were punctuated by the dip of oars. As he heard the speakers outside, Dick's mind suddenly realized who "W. M." was.

"What a chump I was not to think of it before!" he exclaimed. "It's William Masterson, of course, and that's his voice outside. Gee whillakers, they must have camped here on purpose to spy on us."

Just then it occurred to Dick that he was, as a matter of fact, spying on Masterson. He went to the cave door. Below was a boat containing Masterson and his two friends. They had apparently been to town for supplies, for the boat was full of canned goods and provisions.

Just as Dick got to the door Masterson spied the home-made boat lying on the bank at the foot of the cliff.

"Say, fellows," he exclaimed, "somebody's been paying us a call."

"Some thieving Indian, judging from the looks of that boat," said Sam Higgins.

"Well, we're not receiving callers of any kind right now," sputtered Eph angrily.

Dick crouched back into the doorway of the cave. He was trying to think what to do. It was an awkward situation. He didn't want to be caught in what looked, on the face of it, like an act of spying, and yet he didn't wish Masterson and his cronies to think him a coward.

"Say, fellows," spoke up Higgins suddenly, "you don't think it could be one of those kids from the camp below, do you? They may have seen us snooping around there at night and got wise to where we are hiding."

"It had better not be one of them," said Masterson in a loud, threatening voice. "If I catch him, I'll break every bone in his body."

"I guess I'll have a fight on my hands," muttered Dick. "Well, serves me right for butting in," he added philosophically.

"Let's go up and see who it is?" said Eph. "He must be in the cave."

"You go first," said Sam Higgins, who was not over-brave, "it might be a bad man or an Indian."

"Pshaw, I'm not afraid!" said Masterson. "Give me your pistol, Sam, if you're scared."

"I'm not scared, but there's no use running into trouble," said Sam. "Besides I'm kind of lame. I think I—er—wrenched my ankle getting out of the boat."

"I guess you wrenched your nerve," sneered Eph.

Then, headed by Masterson, with the pistol in his grasp, they began to ascend the pathway. Dick was in a quandary. But he decided that the only way to tackle the problem was to take the bull by the horns. As Masterson reached the mouth of the cave the boy dashed out like a redheaded thunderbolt.

Taken utterly by surprise, Masterson stepped back.

Bang!

The pistol went off in the air and the next instant Masterson, despite his efforts to save himself, toppled off the narrow path and went rolling down the bank into the river. Luckily for him, he was a good swimmer, and struck out lustily as he came to the surface.

"Wow!" yelled Dick, and charged like a young buffalo at Eph.

Young Compton tried to strike him but Dick, with lowered head, charged him in the stomach. With a grunt Eph fell back, and in his fall knocked over Sam Higgins, just behind him.

"Whoop-ee!" shouted Dick, rejoicing in his triumph. He leaped over the recumbent forms of Eph and Sam and dashed down the path to the place where he had beached his boat.

He jumped on board and poled off just as young Masterson reached the shore and pulled himself out of the water.

"You infernal young spy!" shrieked Masterson, beside himself with rage, "I'll get even with you for this, see if I don't!"

Sam and Eph, who had picked themselves up, shouted other threats at Dick. But he turned round and, with a pleasant smile, waved a hand as the current carried his boat round the bend. He felt in high good humor at the way he had gotten out of a difficult situation. It was fortunate for him, though, that he had taken Masterson and his cronies so utterly by surprise, otherwise the adventure might have had a different conclusion.

He had established one fact, however, and that was that Masterson and the others were spying on them every night and watching every step in their preparations for the departure for Rattlesnake Island.

That night a strict watch was kept in the camp, all the adventurers taking turns at sentry duty. But nobody came near the place.

CHAPTER XXVII

THE PROFESSOR'S SECOND DILEMMA

Early the next day old man McGee paid them a call. He came to take back the burro they had hired from him for convenience in getting back and forth from Yuma. He also wanted to get a ladder which had been left at the deserted shanty. The old man rode into camp on a razor-backed horse and professed great astonishment when he saw how nearly completed the work on the Wondership was.

"But you kain't fool me," he said knowingly. "I may be old but I'm wise. That thing fly? Why, you might as well tell me the Nat'nul Hotel in Yuma could go kerflopping about in the air. By the way," he went on, "frum ther talk in ther town you ain't ther only ones as is goin' down ther river. There's three young chaps has bought two boats and allows that they're fixin' to take a trip."

"Is that so?" exclaimed Jack with a significant look at his chums. "I think we can guess who they are."

But old man McGee was busy fussing with the donkey and didn't hear him. He was going to carry the ladder back to town on the little creature's back. He lashed the ladder across the saddle so that it stuck out on both sides of the burro, who viewed the proceedings with a kind of mild surprise. It brayed loudly and flapped its long ears in a way that made the boys laugh heartily.

"There," said old man McGee at last, "that's done. Now I reckon I'll bid you so-long and good-luck, and be on my way. When are you goin' ter start?"

"To-morrow morning," replied Jack, "if everything is all right."

"Hold on a minute," said Tom suddenly, as old man McGee was riding off. "I've got a notion for some rabbit pie. Give me the rifle, Dick, and I'll go a little way with Mr. McGee, as far as that little willow wood where you got the cotton-tails."

"All right," said Dick, "and tell you what I'll do. I'll come, too. I can borrow Jack's rifle."

"It's in the tent," said Jack. "Take good care of it."

"I'll do that," promised Dick.

Jack and Zeb went back to their task of putting the finishing touches on the Wondership, stocking her lockers with provisions for the Rattlesnake Island trip, while old man McGee, accompanied by the two boys, rode out of the camp.

The professor was away collecting specimens somewhere and had not been seen since breakfast time.

The donkey, carrying its odd burden, walked behind old McGee's horse and the boys kept pace alongside, listening to the old prospector's everlasting stories of how some day he would strike it rich. His faith never wavered. He believed implicitly that eventually he would make the "big strike" and live in affluence for the remainder of his life.

The willow grove, where Dick went rabbit-hunting, was up the river and on its banks far away from the water nothing grew but cactus, greasewood and mesquite. As they neared it the monotony of the walk began to pall on Dick. He wanted to have some fun.

He fell behind and took a magnifying glass from his pocket. It was one he used in his photographic work. Holding it up he focused the sun's rays through it so that they fell in a tiny burning spot on the donkey's back. After a few seconds the heat burned through. The donkey gave a loud bray and kicked up its heels wildly.

Before old man McGee knew what was happening, the creature had jerked the rope by which he was leading it out of the old man's hand and dashed off toward the willow wood.

"Hey, come back, consarn ye!" shouted old McGee. "What's the matter with ther critter, anyhow? He's gone plum daffy."

Dick, doubled up with laughter, watched the circus. There was the donkey with the ladder across its back racing at full speed toward the wood, and after it came old McGee on his bony old horse, shouting at the top of his voice.

Straight for the wood the donkey raced, kicking up its heels and braying loudly. It dashed in among the trees of the willow wood and at the same instant there came an appalling yell from among the trees.

"Gracious, what's happened now!" gasped Tom, and then catching Dick's laughing eye, he exclaimed:

"Dick, this is some of your work!"

"Maybe," said Dick, still choking with laughter, "but what on earth is happening in the wood?"

"Help! Lions! Help! They're after me! Help!"

The cries came thick and fast.

"It's the professor," choked out Dick.

"He says there are lions in there," cried Tom, looking rather alarmed, but at this juncture something happened to the donkey that momentarily distracted their attention. In trying to pass between two saplings the animal had bumped the ladder against them and brought itself up with a round turn. But it still struggled forward and kept up its braying:

"Cotched, by ginger!" shouted old man McGee. He galloped toward the runaway donkey, but the next moment a curious thing happened.

In pressing forward, the donkey had bent the saplings over with the ladder until it became entangled in their branches. Suddenly the animal ceased struggling and the saplings sprang up, no longer having any pressure on them, and the donkey was fairly lifted from its feet and carried up into the air. And there he hung, threshing about with his hoofs and suspended from the ladder. At the same instant the figure of the professor emerged from the wood. He looked rather sheepish.

The boys ran up to him.

"What's the matter, professor?" asked Dick.

"Yes, you called for help," added Tom.

"Um—er—ah did I call?" inquired the man of science.

"You certainly did. You scared us almost to death," said Dick.

"Something about lions," added Tom.

"Lions—er—did I say *lions*, boys?"

"You did," Dick assured him.

The professor gave a rather shamefaced smile. He looked at the donkey suspended from the ladder between the two straightened saplings.

"Um—er—perhaps it would be better to say no more about it," he said. "I do not suppose that I am the first man to have been scared by a sheep in wolf's clothing."

"Or a donkey in a lion's skin," chuckled Dick.

In the meantime old man McGee had arrived at the donkey's side and was scratching his head to think of some way to relieve it from its predicament. The boys solved the problem for him by cutting the branches that held the ladder and Mr. Donkey came down to earth. The professor, with rather a red face, had gone back to his work of collecting specimens, which the arrival of the long-eared beast had interrupted in such a startling manner.

"Thar, I hope that's taught you some sense," said old man McGee, as the donkey was once more on terra firma. As he rode off, Dick burst into shouts of laughter. His little joke had certainly turned out to be better than he expected and for many days after that he had only to slyly introduce some talk about a lion to cause the professor to look at him in a very quizzical way.

CHAPTER XXVIII

THE UPPER REGIONS

The boys were up with the sun the next day. It was the morning which was to witness the start of the flight for Rattlesnake Island. Everything about the Wondership was in readiness for the enterprise, and there only remained the tin breakfast utensils and the tents to be packed when they had concluded the morning meal.

Naturally excitement ran high. The hunt for the island, too, might be a long one. But they felt that ultimately they would find it, that it would not be like the three buttes of Peg-leg Smith.

When everything was declared ready, Jack opened the charging-tube of the gas reservoir and poured in some of the volatile powder that made the lifting vapor. In fifteen minutes the gauge showed a good pressure in the tank and the valve was turned.

In the hot sun the balloon bag expanded quickly. At length the bag was almost full.

"Everything ready?" cried Jack, at length, when all were on board.

"Ready," said Tom at the engines.

"Then off we go!"

Tom pulled the clutch lever and the propellers whirled. Jack gave the steering and controlling wheel an impulse and like a huge bird the Wondership shot up. But she rose slowly, for besides the unusual number of passengers, she was also carrying a great weight in supplies.

As the craft rose three figures watched it from under the concealment of a clump of mesquite.

"There they go, boys," said Masterson, for it was he and his two cronies.

"Yes, they're off for Rattlesnake Island," sneered Eph. "I hope they get bitten."

"I'll bet they don't dream that we know everything about their plans," chuckled Sam. "I'd like to get even with that red-headed kid."

"Well, you'll get a chance before long," declared Bill Masterson. "I don't see that there's any use in hanging around here any longer," he went on. "The thing to do now is to get our boats and go down the river."

"Won't they be astonished when they see us," said Eph.

"Maybe they'll try to chase us away. They outnumber us," said the timid Sam.

"They'd better not," vaunted Bill Masterson. "I guess we've got as good a right to that old island as they have."

"That's right," echoed Eph, following his leader's sentiments. "I guess they haven't got any mortgage on it."

Viewed from the Wondership, the desert spread out below was a wonderful panorama. Through it, like a deep wound, the

Colorado cut its way and far beyond were the pale, misty outlines of mountains. As they flew onward, the character of the scenery began to change.

The river appeared to sink, while mighty walls, of most gorgeous colors, cliffed it in. The rocks glowed with red and yellow and blue like a painter's palate. But this was only in the deep canyon. On either side the desert, vast and unlimited, stretched away grayly to the horizon.

"It must have taken centuries for the river to have cut such a deep valley," said Tom, looking down as they flew far above it.

"Some say that the river didn't cut it," said Zeb. "They claim that there was a big earthquake or some sort of a shake-up, and that made that big hole in the ground."

Below them they could see birds circling above the swiftly racing waters flecked with white foam. So far no sign of land answering the description of Rattlesnake Island had come in view. But several small, isolated spots of land were encountered, and on one, which looked something like Rattlesnake Island described on the map, they descended.

The boys were delighted at the way the great Wondership settled down into the canyon and then came to rest on the back of the island round which the water rushed and roared. They scattered and ran about on it, enjoying the opportunity to stretch their legs.

Jack, Tom and Dick took a rifle along with them and they were glad they had done so, for as they made their way through a patch of brush a beautiful deer sprang out and dashed off. Jack had the rifle at his shoulder in a minute and the creature bounded into the air, as the crack of the report sounded, and then fell dead.

The boy felt some remorse at having killed it, but he knew they would be in need of fresh meat and some venison would be a welcome addition to the ordinary camp fare. The boys carried the deer back and Zeb skillfully skinned and quartered it. While he was doing this, the boys speculated as to how the animal could have come to the island.

Zeb set their discussion at rest by explaining that it had probably swum the rapids to escape a mountain lion or a lynx. He said that he had often shot deer under similar conditions. As it was almost noon, they decided to wait on the island till they had eaten lunch. Zeb sliced off some venison cutlets and cooked them to a turn over hot wood coals. The boys thought they had never tasted anything better than the fresh meat.

While the plates and knives and forks were being washed and put away, the professor wandered off on his perennial quest of rocks and specimens. He said that he would be back in a short time but was anxious not to miss the opportunity of finding some possibly rare stones.

But everything was ready and the boys were waiting impatiently half an hour later, and there was no sign of the professor.

Suddenly they heard his voice shouting to them from the distance.

"What's he saying?" asked Jack.

"Hark!" admonished Tom.

The professor's shouts came plainly to their ears the next minute, borne on a puff of wind that swept through the canyon.

"Help! Help!" was the burden of his cries. "Get me out!"

"Now, what's happened to him?" demanded Zeb, with a trace of impatience.

"I don't know, but he must be in trouble of some sort," cried Jack.

"Maybe it's another donkey," mischievously suggested Dick.

The cries were redoubled. They waited no longer but started off across the island on the run. Zeb carried his big forty-four revolver.

CHAPTER XXIX

A MUD BATH

The ground was rough and rocky but they made good time. Bursting through a screen of trees from beyond which came the professor's piteous cries, they received a shock.

The man of science was in the center of a large, round hole full of black mud that bubbled and boiled and steamed as if it were alive. All that was visible of the professor was the upper part of his body.

Seriously alarmed, the boys shouted to him to keep up his courage, and that they would get him out.

"How did you get in?" asked Zeb, cupping his hands.

"I fell in," rejoined the poor professor. "The ground gave way under my feet. Hurry and get me out, it's terribly hot."

They looked about them desperately for some means of extricating him from his predicament. But just at the moment none was offered, and with every struggle the professor was sinking deeper in the black, evil-smelling pool of mud.

"Gracious, what are we to do?" cried Jack in despair.

"He's too far out to reach him," said Zeb, equally at a loss.

"But we must do something," chimed in Tom.

Suddenly Zeb had an inspiration. A tree grew on the banks of the mud volcano, the sudden caving in of which, under the professor's weight, had precipitated him into it.

"If I could get out on that branch," said Zeb, "I might be able to bend it enough to bring my feet over him and then work back toward the edge of the mudhole."

"It's worth trying—anything is worthy trying," agreed Jack.

Zeb took off his coat and then shinned up the tree. Then, hanging by his hands he began working out along the branch. As he went it bent till it hung right over the mudhole. Before long his feet dangled above the professor's head.

"Now then, professor," panted Zeb, "take hold on my feet and work along toward the edge of the hole with me."

The professor seized Zeb's boots with the grasp of a drowning man. The branch cracked ominously.

"Easy thar, professor," warned Zeb earnestly. "Don't pull more'n you can help or we'll both be in the soup."

The professor lightened his grip and slowly, hand over hand, Zeb began the slow journey back along the branch. It was a feat only possible to a man whose muscles were of iron. And before it was over even Zeb was almost overcome. Perspiration streamed from his forehead and soaked his shirt as he dropped from the branch, having accomplished the journey and pulled the professor to the bank.

"That's what I call toeing a man out of trouble," punned Dick, in the general relief that followed.

"Good thing it warn't no further," puffed Zeb, mopping his forehead. "My arms feels as if they'd been stretched on one of them racks you read about in the history books."

"How did it happen, professor?" asked Jack, as they scraped the mud off the scientist.

"It's hard to say," was the response. "I was walking along, intent on my collecting, when I came to a barren patch of ground that was crusted over with stuff that looked like salt. I stepped out on it to investigate and suddenly in I went. Faugh! how it smells."

"Yes, it isn't exactly perfumed," said Jack. "But how did such a place come there?"

"It's one of those mud-springs of hot water that are found in several places throughout the West," said the scientist. "It must have been quiescent for some time and then the thin skin of alkaline earth formed over it. In Europe, or if we had that spring near a large city, it would be possible to make a fortune with it."

"In what way?" asked Dick.

"As a curative bath," replied the professor. "Every year people spend fortunes to go to Europe and take just such baths."

"Reckon I'd go without washin' then," commented Zeb.

"I'd just as soon bathe in rotten eggs," said Dick.

"Well," said Jack, "I guess we've got off about all the mud we can for the present. We'd better be getting back. It's mighty fortunate that we came in time."

"Yes, I was slipping into the stuff all the time," said the professor. "If I'd been alone on the island I might have never been seen again," he added in quite a matter-of-fact tone. "It's too bad I lost that bag of fossils, though. I had some fine specimens."

"Goodness, no wonder you sank down!" exclaimed Jack. "Why didn't you let go of them?"

The scientist was mildly surprised.

"Why, how could I," he asked, "until it became a question of life or death? It's too bad I had to lose them," and he shook his head mournfully at the thought.

The journey was soon resumed, the Wondership rising buoyantly out of the dismal canyon. They were not sorry to get back to the upper air for the gloom of the deep gulch had affected their spirits. But so much time had been consumed in getting the professor out of his predicament that it was not long before twilight set in and they still had caught no glimpse of anything resembling the island they were in search of.

They decided to come to earth and make camp for the night and resume the search in the morning. They made a hearty supper off the venison which remained, and turned in, without setting any watch, as there was no necessity for it out there with not a soul about for scores of miles.

It was about midnight when Jack was awakened by a wild yell from Tom.

"Ow! Ouch! Leggo my toe!" the younger of the Boy Inventors was shouting.

CHAPTER XXX

NIGHT ON THE COLORADO

"What's the matter? What has happened?" cried Jack.

"Is it Indians?" cried Dick, who had a lively imagination.

"Something grabbed my foot," declared Tom.

"Grabbed your foot?" repeated Jack.

"Well, maybe, nibbled at it, would be better," replied Tom. "It isn't hurt, but I was awakened by it. I guess the thing, whatever it was, must have been scared away."

"What could it have been?" came from Dick.

"Perhaps it was a bear," suggested Tom.

"A bear, nonsense. I guess it was all imagination," scoffed Jack. "You ate too much at supper, Tom."

"It was not imagination, I tell you," retorted Tom indignantly. "I felt it just as plainly as anything."

"Well, I don't see what—" began Jack and then he broke off.

From outside the tent had come an appalling crash of tin dishes, followed by unearthly grunts and squeals. The uproar was terrific. It sounded as if every piece of tinware in the camp was being hurled and battered around.

"What under the sun—?" gasped Jack.

"It's Indians; they've attacked the camp," cried Dick.

A weird screech split the night. Jack seized up a rifle.

"Come on, boys," he cried, but it might have been noticed that Dick was not particularly alert in following.

Zeb and the professor rushed out of their tents and their shouts added to the confusion. There was a bright moon and by its light Jack saw a small, peculiarly-shaped animal charging about blindly here and there. The next minute he saw, too, that the creature's head was caught fast in an enameled cooking pot.

It rushed about and uttered the muffled squeals that had attracted their attention. Jack raised his rifle and fired. The creature fell dead at the first shot. Zeb and Jack rushed up to it.

"A badger!" exclaimed Zeb, "and he's got his greedy head stuck fast in that mush cooker."

"And in charging about trying to get it off he'd made a wreck of our pantry!" exclaimed Jack, looking at the tin utensils scattered in every direction about the wooden box in which they were kept.

"It must have been that badger that came sniffing at my toes," said Tom.

"Or maybe it was Indians," laughed Jack, looking slyly at Dick, who was glad that they couldn't see how red he turned.

"Indians?" exclaimed the professor guilelessly. "Were there any

Indians about?"

"Dick thought he saw some," explained Jack with a chuckle.

The dead badger was pulled out of the pot into which it stuck its head to lick out the remains of some oatmeal that had adhered to its side, and the boys went back to bed. But they did not sleep much after the uproar into which the camp had been thrown, and were glad when it began to grow light.

Zeb cooked a fine breakfast to which he urged everybody to do justice, as they had a long and possibly a trying day ahead of them. The badger was given decent burial by Dick.

"Let its fate be a lesson to you," said Jack, at which they all laughed, for Dick was always on the spot at meal times.

When the morning meal was finished and the things all packed away, the Wondership was inflated and soared into the clear air. Nights and early mornings on the desert are cool, and it was crisp and invigorating in the hours before the sun had risen high. But by noon the heat grew blistering, and they were still soaring above the river without a trace of Rattlesnake Island being visible.

However, that afternoon they sighted a group of islands of which the largest at once attracted their attention. A prominent feature of Rattlesnake Island, as outlined on the map, was a big dead pine, situated like a beacon, at the summit of the peak into which the island rose.

The river at this point broadened out. Great cliffs overhung it. They were made up of strata of brilliant colors. It looked from above as if they had been painted by some titanic sign painter—nature, the artist.

Jack was the first to call attention to the island which had caught his eye while he scanned the river below them with the binoculars. He at once noticed its formation, long and narrow, with a high, rocky peak rising out from amongst trees and bushes which clothed it almost to the summit.

Then his eye caught a great white pine trunk, standing like a flagpole almost at the apex of the peak.

"Hurrah, boys!" he cried. "I guess that's the place. Welcome to Rattlesnake Island!"

Tom was steering, "spelling" Jack at the wheel.

"You can see the island?" he demanded.

"Yes, or if it isn't it, it's like enough to be its twin brother."

Everybody began to get excited. Zeb took the glasses and after a careful scrutiny and a reference to the map, declared that the island below them tallied in every way with its description.

"Then down we go," said Jack.

"All right," nodded Tom, who was almost as good an air pilot as his cousin.

The Wondership dropped rapidly. Soon they were mmediately above the island, which was now seen to be rocky and precipitous, except at one end where there was a great open place, bare and desolate looking.

On the edges of this cleared spot, which looked swampy and unwholesome, were serried rows of trees, every one of which was dead as if from a blight, and offering with their gaunt, leafless branches a sharp contrast to the green leafiness of the rest of the island.

Jack scanned the place sharply as they dropped down and Tom prepared to land on the edge of the swamp. As they got closer to the ground, he suddenly became aware of something that caused him a sharp shock of surprise.

"Why there's somebody on the island!" he exclaimed.

"Somebody on the island?" echoed Zeb incredulously.

"Yes, or at least there's a dwelling place."

The boy pointed to a rude sort of shack built of logs and roofed with boughs, which stood on the edge of the cleared space.

"Great Methuselah!" ejaculated Zeb. "Can someone have stolen a march on us?"

"I don't know, but it looks queer, and see, there's a shovel. Somebody has been digging here."

"But who could it be?" demanded Tom, mystified.

"Gosh! Looks as if we've bin euchered after all," grumbled Zeb.

The Wondership came to earth at the edge of the lifeless-looking, bare space. They clambered out of the machine and stood on what was, undoubtedly, Rattlesnake Island, for every landmark on the map had been verified as they dropped.

They looked about them for a minute and then Zeb drew his revolver out of the holster and began idly twiddling the cylinder.

"I want ter make sure she's in workin' order," he said with a grim comprehension of the lips, "before we do any investigating."

CHAPTER XXXI

THE ISLAND OF MYSTERY

There was an air of oppression, hard to explain, about the island. But they all felt it. The boys were inclined to talk in whispers and even Dick Donovan's usual lively spirits seemed daunted. There was something about the blistered, barren look of the cleared space on the edge of which they had landed that gave them all an odd feeling of melancholy.

Zeb was the first to shake this off.

"Our first job," he said, "is to find out who is on the island and what they've been doing."

Here and there in the black, swampy-looking bare space, they could see where holes had been dug, but when they examined the spade, which Jack had seen from the Wondership as they descended, they found that it was rusty and had evidently not been used for a long time.

It was the same in the rude hut which they examined. Some rusty utensils and a few ragged old garments were all that was inside. The dust lay thick on the floor and a large squirrel leaped out of the roof as they entered.

"Well, whoever was on the island has moved on again," declared Zeb.

"Or died," said Jack in a low tone.

"Wa'al, what I say is," observed Zeb, "ther sooner we git at that what-yer-may-call-um stuff and get away agin, the better it'll be for all of us. There's suthin' about this island I don't like."

The others agreed, all except the professor, who, on hands and knees, was examining some rocks with his magnifying glass.

"Where shall we make camp?" asked Dick.

"I don't much fancy this side of the island, somehow," said Jack, "but we could pitch the tents on that little plateau up there and be comfortable and have a good view up and down the river at the same time."

And so it was arranged. Leaving the Wondership on the edge of the clearing, they made camp on the flat ledge of sandy soil interspersed with rocks that Jack had selected. From it they had a good view in both directions. Above them was a small island, and below them the river leaped and roared in a series of big rapids.

Their preparations for camping occupied all the afternoon. It was supper time when they had finished and everything was shipshape and comfortable. In the meantime Dick had wandered off with the rifle and returned with four good-sized rabbits and three squirrels which Zeb cooked into a savory stew.

They turned in early as they had all worked hard and were tired. Just what time it was that he awakened, Jack did not know. But he thought it was after midnight. Taking his watch he went to the door of the tent to look at it in the moonlight, as he did not wish to arouse the others by striking a light.

The moon flooded the island. Jack looked about him, enjoying the beauty of the scene. The cliffs were great masses of black and white and the rushing river gleamed like silver. He glanced toward the black waste, on the edge of which they left the Wondership. The next instant he uttered a startled exclamation. Above the bare patch of dark-colored earth tall white figures were dancing, gleaming in the moonlight.

Jack's heart gave a bound and he caught his breath for an instant. Then he felt inclined to laugh at his own fears. What he had taken for ghostly figures were columns of vapor writhing and twisting as they steamed upward from the bare end of the island. What caused them, Jack did not know. He noticed, too, that the whole patch of barren land glowed with a strange phosphorescence like rotted wood.

Fascinated by the spectacle, he stood gazing at it. There was something eerie about the dancing, pirouetting columns of vapor. They looked like a party of ghosts dancing a quadrille. They twisted and contorted and bowed and soared upward and sank again in a kind of rhythm.

"Gracious, this is a spooky sort of place," thought Jack. "I wonder what causes those wavering columns? Maybe some sort of hidden hot springs like the one the professor fell into. I know one thing, I don't like this island overmuch. As Zeb said, there is something queer about it—something in the air. I don't know what, but I for one won't be sorry when we leave it."

He fell to musing about his father waiting so many miles away for news of the discovery that was to rehabilitate his fortunes and place the radio telephone in the list of practical inventions that have created an epoch in the world's history.

"Poor old dad," he thought "After all, he's really having the most trying part of this thing. Waiting back there for he doesn't know what, and with nothing to do but wait. I wonder if we are going to succeed? We will, we must! But, supposing that the map was wrong and that—"

His musing broke off suddenly and he crouched forward watching intently. His eyes were staring wide-open and startled at the Wondership. Its bulk lay blackly against the faint, phosphorescent glow of the black barren.

Then he felt his scalp tighten and his mouth go dry while his heart seemed to stop for an instant and then pound furiously, shaking his frame.

For a second he had seen something that had almost startled him into a cry. A dark figure was creeping round the Wondership, crouched like an ape as it examined the craft.

The boy had hardly caught a glimpse of it before it vanished, gliding swiftly like an animal into the brush. Jack rubbed his eyes.

"Am I seeing things?" he asked himself, "but no, I'm positive, as sure as I stand here, that that was a human figure sneaking about down there. Who could it have been?"

Jack did not sleep much more that night. The thought that they were not alone on the island was a disquieting one.

CHAPTER XXXII

THROUGH THE WOODS

The next morning Jack watched his opportunity, and under the pretext of hunting, left camp after breakfast and made his way to the side of the Wondership. He wanted to examine the vicinity for footmarks. But he found none, which was not surprising, for the ground on which the craft had been brought to rest was hard and firm, and not likely to take on any impressions.

In the bright, sunny glow it was hard for the boy to believe that he had actually seen the mysterious figure in the moonlight. But although he tried to assure himself that he had been the victim of an illusion, and that he had mistaken the shadow of a waving tree branch for a man, Jack knew that he was not laboring under a mistake. He was certain he had seen rightly; but he decided, for the present, to say nothing to his companions about the events of the night.

Having failed to find any tracks round the Wondership, he started off through the trees on his hunt. He was traversing a small glade when, in a clump of flowering bushes, he heard a sudden scuffling noise.

Startled, he stopped. The sound came again and this time it was accompanied by a shrill scream as of some creature in pain. Jack parted the bushes and made his way through them. On the other side he came across a rabbit. The little creature was struggling violently and squealing with the peculiarly human screech that rabbits have when in pain.

The boy saw that it had been caught in some way and could not get away. Greatly mystified, he dropped to his knees beside it and the next instant solved the puzzle.

The rabbit was caught in a trap ingeniously made from pliable willow twigs and set in a "rabbit run." For a minute the full significance of his discovery did not dawn upon Jack. Then it came like a bolt from the blue.

Somebody on the island, other than themselves, had set that trap! Perhaps it was the strange, half-ape-like man he had seen by the Wondership the night before. The boy looked round him in the silent wood as if he half expected to see somebody watching him.

He was not afraid, but he felt that creepy feeling that accompanies the mysterious. Suddenly he recollected that he had left his rifle behind when he plunged into the bushes.

He remembered this when the desire came to him to put the rabbit out of its misery. It had been caught by the hind leg and had wrenched it out of joint in its frantic struggles to get free. Jack made his way back to where he had left his rifle. But when he got back to the trap ready to end the poor creature's life, the rabbit was not there!

The trap was empty!

Then he looked about him. The ground was covered with blood and fur as if the rabbit had been torn to pieces.

"Some animal," was his first thought. Then, on examining the trap, he found that the thong which had ensnared the rabbit had not been broken or torn loose as would have been the case had some wild creature pounced on the rabbit and dragged it off.

It had been untied!

Jack had just made this discovery when he noticed something fluttering from a thornbush. He was sure it had not been there before, for he had noted the surroundings of the trap carefully. He examined the object that had caught his attention. It was a bit of canvas, seemingly torn from a garment made of that material.

"There *is* somebody else on the island!" gasped Jack, looking round with white cheeks.

He clutched his rifle firmly. Looking about him he half expected to see some wild face peering at him out of parted bushes. But nothing of the sort happened. Feeling very uncomfortable, Jack came away from the place and made his way back to camp.

This time he made up his mind to confide in Zeb. The prospector was as mystified as Jack over the events of the night and the incident of the rabbit trap. But he was unable to throw any light on the affair.

"It might be an Indian," he said, "or—"

"It might be the man that built that hut and left the shovel sticking in that barren place down yonder," said Jack.

"In that case, wouldn't he be livin' in ther hut instead of snoopin' round the island?" asked Zeb.

This view seemed to be incontrovertible. At noon the professor, who had been scouting over the island looking for specimens which might give him some clue as to the mineral deposits they had come in search of, arrived in camp breathless and indignant.

"A joke's a joke," he said to the boys, "but this is going too far."

"What's the matter, professor?" asked Dick.

"Yes, what's happened?" asked Tom, who saw that the man of science was really angry, and for some reason blamed them for whatever had irritated him.

"As if you didn't know," declared the professor. "I set my bag of specimens down on a rock while I went to investigate a peculiar-looking formation."

"Well?" said Jack.

"Well, I heard a soft footstep and the crackling of some twigs. I looked round and my bag of specimens had gone. Now which of you boys played that foolish joke on me?"

"I'll give you my word we know nothing about it, professor," declared Tom. "Dick and I have been working all the morning unpacking stuff from the Wondership."

The professor looked at them incredulously.

"That's right," struck in Zeb, "they haven't been out of my sight."

"But—but," stammered the professor, "my dear sir, that bag of specimens didn't walk off, you know. Besides," he added, "I heard a human footfall distinctly."

"It may not have been the boys, though," spoke up Jack seriously.

"Indeed, who else then?" inquired the professor stiffly.

"An unwelcome neighbor," replied Jack. "We are not alone on this island."

"Not alone? What do you mean?" demanded the professor in thunderstruck tones.

"Just this, that there is someone else on it. Who or what it is I don't know."

And Jack went on to explain all that he had seen.

CHAPTER XXXIII

THE SECRET AT LAST

Mysteries are always uncomfortable. As Jack proceeded with his narrative, Dick and Tom looked nervously about them. Even the boys' two elders looked grave. The presence of a man on the island was almost inexplicable. But Jack's story was so circumstantial that there was no room to suppose that he might be mistaken. Besides, he had the bit of canvas to show, the scrap that he had taken from the thornbush.

After dinner Tom and Dick resumed their work of unloading necessaries from the Wondership. Jack and the two elder members of the party discussed plans.

"You haven't found any trace of mineral-bearing rock yet, have you, professor?" asked Jack.

The professor shook his head.

"Not a speck of anything that even remotely corresponds with the black sand that Zeb brought East with him," said the man of science, dejectedly.

"It isn't possible that we have been fooled," said Zeb.

"Or landed on the wrong island," struck in Jack.

"It must be the right island," declared Zeb.

"How do you make that out?" asked Jack.

"Well, it's got every mark on it that the map gives, for one thing," said Zeb.

"That's so," agreed the professor, and then he added hopefully: "However, I haven't covered half the ground yet."

Tom and Dick came tramping back at that juncture. They carried some canned goods and Dick bore the rusty shovel that they had seen the day before sticking up in the black barren.

"It was sticky and moist out there," he said, "but I figured we could always use this shovel, so I went out and brought it along."

He flung himself down full length in the shade for it was hot and there was not a breath of wind to fan the canyon. The professor, who sat facing Dick, concentrated his attention for an instant on the soles of the youngster's boots. Then he leaped up with a yell that startled them.

"What is it? The wild man?" gasped Dick, looking round him in alarm.

"No, your boots, your boots; look at them!" cried the professor.

"Is there a snake on them?" cried Dick, preparing to jump up.

"Don't move! Don't move for your life!" fairly screamed the dumpy little geologist, springing forward. He fell on his knees at Dick's boots as if they had been sacred, and with trembling fingers flaked off, into his left palm, some black mud which stuck to them.

Then he stood erect, his face aglow with triumph and enthusiasm such as the man of science rarely permitted himself.

"Gentlemen," he said, with a flourish, "there is no reason to look further for the mineral-bearing ground."

"You have found it?" choked out Jack.

"Yes."

"Where?"

"On Dick Donovan's boots."

They looked at him as if they thought he had suddenly gone demented. Dick examined his boots carefully as if he expected to see money plastered all over them.

The professor extended his palm. In it lay the black earth he had scraped from Dick's boots. In it tiny particles glittered and gleamed like myriads of infinitesimal eyes.

"Z. 2. X.," said the professor in solemn tones, and he waved his hand down toward the black barren where the moist, unhealthy-looking bare patch lay quivering and sweltering in the sun. A kind of haze hung above it, like a very thin fog.

"There it is," he went on, "down there. Waiting to be extracted from that black earth. Look."

He shook the black earth from his palm. Where it had lain there was a red, irritated-looking patch. The professor showed it. It looked like a slight burn.

"Did that stuff do it?" asked Jack.

"Yes; and that's almost as definite a proof as an analysis, of its intense radio activity. You noticed that the sample that Zeb had was enclosed in a leaden tube. That was the reason. Such powerful stuff would inflict bad burns if not handled properly."

"So that was why you made us include asbestos gloves and foot coverings and black goggles in the outfit?" cried Tom, who had been much puzzled over the reason for that part of the equipment.

"That was why," said the professor, "and that also is the reason we brought along those lead containers. Z. 2. X. or its ally, radium, or in fact vanadium or any of the allied radio-active metals, would destroy any other sort of container."

"Let's go down now and start digging," suggested impulsive Dick.

"Don't venture out there till you are fully equipped for the job," said the professor. "Serious results might ensue. In the meantime, I am going to analyze this sample in order to be doubly sure."

Jack gave a deep sigh of relief. After all, it was not a dream. They had found the valuable earth. It was now only a question of transportation. His father's fortunes were saved. The radio-'phone would be rushed to perfection and placed on the market within a short time of their return home.

While Jack lay back and indulged in daydreams, the others watched the professor as he tested the black sand over a portable assaying furnace and made all sorts of experiments to determine its value and the proportion of the different precious metals contained in it.

There was a slight rustling in the bushes behind him. Jack, whose nerves had been rather on edge since the occurrences of the preceding night and that morning, faced round quickly.

The next instant he uttered a loud shout.

Peering out of the bushes was a hideous, hairy face, more like an ape's than a human being's. From it glowed two wild, piercing eyes, like those of a beast of prey.

As Jack shouted and the others started toward him, the face vanished like a flash.

CHAPTER XXXIV

THE INTERLOPERS

"Well, we'll git ter ther bottom uv this afore we leave ther island," declared Zeb vehemently, "but right now, pussonally, I'm more interested in gitting those lead carboys filled up with Z. 2. X. and gitting away from here."

"So are we," said Jack, thinking of his father.

They all donned their asbestos gloves and foot coverings under the professor's directions and put on the huge black goggles that had been brought along at the scientist's directions.

"I guess we'd scare that wild man into conniption fits if he could see us now," chuckled Tom, surveying his mates as they started out for the black barren.

"Yes, we look like a lot of men from Mars," agreed Dick.

Armed with shovels they attacked the dark, soft earth at a place the professor indicated. For an hour or more they worked and filled three of the lead carboys. Then Jack spoke.

"It's queer," he said, "but I begin to feel terribly tired, and I haven't worked long, either."

"So do I," said Tom. "I don't feel as if I could lift another shovelful."

"I'm all in," added Dick, throwing down his spade.

"Same here. Jes' 'bout tuckered out," chimed in Zeb.

"It's the effect of the stuff we are working in," said the professor. "Anyhow, we've done enough for to-day. We'll load the lead carboys on the Wondership and then knock off. I don't want you boys to get sick."

They took the loaded carboys to the grounded craft and the professor sealed and soldered a cover on each of them. Then they went back to the camp. Curiously, as soon as they reached it, the lassitude they had felt while working on the black barren left them. Jack proposed a hunting trip to Tom. Dick said he wanted to write up his notes from which, on their return, he was going to construct a big "story" for his paper.

The two chums struck out across the island. They met with fairly good luck. Jack brought down some rabbits and a partridge. Tom got three partridges and some squirrels. Game appeared to be plentiful on the island and Jack had a theory that at one time it must have been connected with the mainland.

At last their walking brought them out on the upper end of the island facing the smaller spot of land above. As they emerged from the trees, both boys got a big surprise.

Two boats had just been beached there!

"What in the world!" stammered out Jack.

"Who can—" began Tom, when the question was answered. The boys saw three figures coming down to the beach. They, seemingly, had been looking for a camp site.

"It's that fellow, Bill Masterson," explained Jack.

"So it is, and those other two are his cronies. The sneaks,

they've followed us here!" cried Tom indignantly.

"Let's watch from behind these bushes and see what they do," said Jack.

They watched from a place of concealment while the three youths on the island above unloaded the second boat which they had towed down the river, carrying their camping equipment and provisions in it. They set up their tents quite boldly in full view of the other island and then proceeded to build a fire.

"How on earth did they get down the river without having a spill?" cried Jack.

"How did they know where Rattlesnake Island was?" wondered Tom, neither of the boys, of course, knowing of the opened letters.

"They seem prepared to make a long stay," commented Tom, after a minute, "but it's a wonder they weren't wrecked."

"I don't know," said Jack. "Zeb says the river is much higher now than he has ever seen it. That means that the rapids are not so dangerous as at low water. But they were taking quite a chance, at that."

The boys watched for a while longer and then returned to camp with their game and their news.

"If they try to land on this island, we'll soon chase 'em off," declared Dick vehemently.

"Then they'd have a case at law agin us," said Zeb.

"How do you mean?" asked Jack.

"Wa'al, we ain't filed no claim yet and in the eyes of the law them deposits down there in the black barren is as much theirs as ours."

That evening Zeb occupied himself with making several signs of intention to file claim which he intended to post all round the black barren, thus marking it off as if it had been a mine. Before they went to bed, Jack and Tom made another excursion to the upper end of the island where they watched the campfires of the interlopers for some time.

Suddenly, while they watched, they saw one of the boats with three figures in it shoved off. The craft began to drop down the river. Masterson, who was at the oars, steered straight for Rattlesnake Island.

"They're going to land here," declared Jack.

"What do you think of that for nerve," gasped Tom.

"The worst of it is, we can't stop them."

"No, that's so. Let's hide behind this rock and see what they do."

The boys slipped behind a big boulder and a moment later the boat was beached.

"Well, here we are," came in Eph's voice, "and if the stuff is worth all you say it is, we ought to get enough out in a couple of nights to make us rich."

"Gee! I can hardly wait till it's time to start digging," said Sam Higgins. "Here we are, on Tom Tiddler's ground, picking up gold and silver."

"Wait till we get it before you start hollering," said Masterson gruffly.

"What time will we start over?" asked Sam.

"About midnight. It will be plenty of time."

"But how are we going to locate it?" objected Eph.

"We can see where they've been digging, can't we?" said Bill Masterson, "or if they haven't started yet, we can hang around and watch till they do."

The three worthies sat under a rock not far from where the boys were and talked. It appeared that Bill Masterson had read up on mining and claim law and knew that the boys could not order them off the island. They had a right to take all of the mineral-bearing earth that they could.

Suddenly, however, their talk stopped.

"What are you doing, Eph?" demanded Sam indignantly.

"Nothing. What do you mean?" asked Eph in an astonished voice.

"You threw a rock at me."

"I didn't."

"You did. Ouch! There's another."

"One hit me, too," cried Eph, springing up, and at the same moment a yell came from Masterson.

Jack and Tom, as much surprised as the three marauders, heard the rocks pelting around them. Suddenly they looked up. Standing on a high rock above the place where Masterson and his cronies were talking, was a strange-looking figure in tattered clothes outlined in the moonlight.

He was busily hurling rocks down at the intruders. Suddenly a demoniacal laugh split the air and the creature vanished, running swiftly, crouched, with long arms hanging.

"It's the wild man!" gasped Tom, while the three worthies on the beach uttered a startled cry.

"It's ghosts, that's what it is," declared Sam Higgins shuddering.

"Nonsense. It's those kids. That's who it is," said Bill, but his voice was rather shaky.

"I never heard anything human laugh like that," declared Eph. "Ugh! it makes my blood run cold."

"Maybe we'd better go back," said Sam. "If we've got a right here I'd just as soon land in the daylight."

"You're a fine pair of babies," growled Bill. "I'm sorry I brought you along. Ghosts indeed—Wow! what was that?"

Another long ringing peal of laughter sounded through the night. It reverberated against the steep walls of the canyon and was flung mockingly from crag to crag. The boys felt their blood chill as they heard it. There was something diabolical in the merriment of the wild man who, they knew, was making the hideous sounds.

"I'm going back to the other island," declared Sam.

"If you move I'll knock your head off," said Masterson. "It's just a trick of those kids to scare us, that's all it is."

CHAPTER XXXV

TRIUMPH

It was midnight. The moon rode high in a cloudless sky, and the camp of the Boy Inventors, to all appearances, was wrapped in slumber. Through the woods came three creeping, cautious figures. Each carried a spade and a sack. They paused by the camp and looked about them.

Then, by the bright moonlight, they saw the bare plateau below. The black barren where the adventurers had been working that afternoon. Masterson was the first to see traces of digging. He seized Eph's arm and pointed.

"That's the place," he said in a hoarse whisper. "See, they've been at work there already."

"Tom Tiddler's ground," whispered Eph.

"I guess we'll get some of it, too," chuckled Sam, who had gotten over his fright in a sudden greed at the thought of riches.

Silently, for they had sacks tied round their feet, the three interlopers crept down the rocky slope toward the black barren. The dark ground, thickly sown with mineral wealth, glittered in the moonlight as if a frost had fallen on it and made it gleam iridescently with millions of sparkling points of light.

As the trio stole down the slope, dark figures from the Boy Inventors' camp followed them. Led by Zeb, they found hiding places and watched operations as Masterson and his cronies began to dig. They wielded their shovels frantically.

"And we can't stop them," groaned Dick.

"Wait a minute," said the professor.

They continued to watch, and before many minutes had passed they saw Sam Higgins lay down his shovel with a grunt.

"Go on and dig," ordered Masterson.

"Yes, hurry up, we haven't got all night," urged Eph.

Sam made a few more feeble movements and then quit.

'"I can't do any more," he said languidly.

"Ouch! my hands are burning," cried Eph suddenly, "and I feel as if all my bones had turned to water. What's the matter with the place?"

After a few minutes more both Eph and Sam gave up, but Masterson stuck doggedly to his task, although his hands were burning terribly, and the radio-active stuff was eating through the sacking on his feet. At last he, too, had to give in. They were too weak to carry the sacks they had partially filled across the island, owing to the effects of the black barren, and staggeringly they hid them to call for them at a later time.

"I thought so," said the professor, as the hidden watchers saw Masterson and the other two wearily clamber up the slope. "They'll have bad sores to-morrow and may be crippled for some time."

"But they'll recover?" said Jack, whose conscience began to smite him.

"Oh, yes, but they will have quite a lesson first," rejoined the professor.

"Let's see what they do next," suggested Jack, and he and Tom carefully made their way to where the trio had left the boat. Masterson ordered Sam to get on board; but just as the timorous youth was about to obey another hideous laugh from near at hand startled him so that he almost jumped out of his skin.

He leaped forward, but in his alarm missed the boat and gave it a shove that sent it into the stream. Sam fell flat on his face, while Masterson, with an exclamation of dismay, leaped for the boat. But the swift current had it in its grasp and bore it rapidly away. Masterson sprang on Sam and began beating him violently as the cause of all the trouble. It was serious' enough for them. The loss of the boat had marooned them on the island.

The boat drifted past a rocky point further down the island shore. Had they been there, they would have been able to seize it. They watched it with alarmed eyes as it sailed down the current. All at once a dark figure dashed from the trees and made a spring from a high rock, hoping, seemingly, to land in the boat. Instead, there was the sound of a heavy fall and then a piteous groan.

Whoever it was had jumped for the boat, had missed it and fallen on the rocks. Not caring whether Masterson and his cronies saw them or not, the boys raced along the beach. From the groans of the injured person they knew that he was badly, possibly mortally, hurt.

In a few minutes they reached his side.

"It's the wild man!" cried Jack, as they gazed at a hairy, wild-looking man who lay stretched out, breathing heavily, on the rocks where he had fallen. His only clothing was a pair of tattered canvas trousers and a ragged shirt.

"Poor old Foxy. He's done for at last, is Foxy, for his sins," groaned the man in an insane voice. "He suffered terrible for his crimes, has Foxy, but it's all over now."

"Foxy!" exclaimed Jack. "That's the man that came down the river with Blue Nose Sanchez. The man who stayed in the boat."

"He must have landed here and then gone crazy from privation," said Jack. "I can't find that any bones are broken," he said after a brief examination. "Suppose we carry him back to camp?"

"I wonder where that Masterson outfit has got to?" said Tom, as they picked up the wasted form of Foxy, who was raving and moaning by turns.

"I don't know. They are in a fine predicament now. They've got no food and no boat They're marooned on this island."

"I suppose we'll have to help them out," said Tom.

"I guess so, though they don't deserve it."

"I lost that boat," moaned Foxy. "I could have got away in it. Poor old Foxy. It's tough on Foxy," and he began to weep.

The professor found that the man had not suffered any broken bones but the fall had bruised and sprained him and he was helpless. From scattered bits of his ravings they learned what he had endured on the island and how, when the black sand began to burn him, he had had to give up working on it. Then his boat had drifted away and since then he had lived the life of a wild man, setting snares for rabbits and partridges, and eating them raw, tearing them with his clawlike fingers.

Early the next day the expected happened. Chastened, and with burned and swollen hands and feet, Masterson and his cronies came into the boys' camp at breakfast time. They looked crestfallen and sheepish, but the boys did not want to make them feel any worse than they did, so they spared them questions at first.

But when Masterson begged them to get them out of their predicament and take them back to Yuma, Jack felt that it was time to put them through a cross examination.

"You followed us here to try to cut out some ground from under our feet, Masterson," he said, "and you know you told me in Nestorville you wanted to get even with me."

"Don't rub it in, Chadwick," said the humbled Masterson. "I'll do anything you say if you'll only get us out of this terrible place. I can hardly walk, and my hands feel as if they'd been burned in a fire."

"How did you know our destination?" asked Tom. Masterson made a full confession and at the end begged forgiveness.

"This ought to be a good lesson to you to mind your own affairs," said Jack as he concluded.

"I know a man who made a big fortune just minding his business," said Dick. "For my part," he went on, "I'll forgive you, but I want you to sign a paper promising not to publish anything about this expedition."

"I will—oh, I will," said Masterson. And then he wrote as Dick dictated. The boys witnessed and signed the paper.

"And now you'd better eat breakfast," said Jack.

Three days later, the Wondership made two trips to Yuma. On the first she took the original party with the addition of the insane Foxy, who was placed in an asylum. He never recovered his reason but died in the institution. Also, there was carried a part of the leaden carboys which they had filled.

Masterson and his cronies had been left behind on the island to pack up the camping equipment and thus make themselves useful. Zeb went to the U.S. Assay Office and formally filed their claim to the island and its riches. In the meantime, the professor took charge of Foxy and turned him over to the authorities.

As for the boys, they sailed back to Rattlesnake Island, after sending a telegram to Mr. Chadwick. It was brief.

"We win," was all it said.

CHAPTER XXXVI

THE HOMECOMING

The next day Masterson and his companions, very much subdued, boarded the Wondership as passengers. All of them were still suffering painfully from the effects of the burns, their only reward from their ill-advised raid on the black barren.

"Boys," asked Masterson, "can't you take our camping equipment along? It's a shame to have it rot here."

"All right," said Jack. "I think we may be able to sell it for you. Come on, we'll get to work now!"

"You're not such a bad chap," said Eph when he heard Jack agree to Masterson's suggestion.

"He's the finest chap on earth!" exclaimed Tom.

"That he is," added Dick Donovan.

"He is a model young man," declared Professor Jenks, overhearing Tom's last remark.

Jack flushed with pleasure and embarrassment. It was very gratifying to know that his friends thought highly of him, but at the same time he wished they would not give him that uneasy feeling with their sincere compliments. So he hurried away, asking the others to follow him toward getting together

Masterson's outfit.

While the dumpy little geologist went once more to search for strange specimens, the boys readily set to work and in a very short time the camping equipment was placed on board the Wondership.

When the boys arrived at Yuma, Masterson found no difficulty in selling the camping outfit to old man McGee, who decided to make one more try to find the Three Buttes.

"Don't you think you're too old, and that the gold, after all, may not be there?" Tom asked the eccentric miner.

"Nonsense!" exclaimed McGee indignantly. "As I tole you afore, it stands ter reason thar's gold out thar, and 'at it war'ent up to Peg-leg Smith nor'n to Guv'nor Downey, nor'n to McGuire, nor'n to Dr. De Courcy, nor'n to any of 'em to find the Buttes, but as I says afore, I says ag'in—'at ther good Lord never made nuthin' thet wasn't of some use. Very well, then, the desert is good fer nuthin' else but mineral wealth, and Providence made it so plagued hard ter git at so 'at all of us couldn't git rich at once. I've been arter the Buttes all me life, and *this* wack I'm goin' to land it rich!"

The fanatical old prospector, chuckling gleefully and sucking his pipe, ambled away while Tom looked after him, shaking his head sympathetically.

"Look out! Look out!" someone shouted in Tom's ear. "There's a beauty, a wonder!"

Tom, startled, whirled about to see the professor, gazing intently at a small rock upon which one of Tom's heels was resting. The professor violently pushed him aside, out came his little hammer, and in a moment the new specimen was in his bag. Then, the man of science, without looking up to see whom he had spoken to, pounced on another stone.

Tom could not help laughing outright at the professor's queer ways and deep concentration on his pet hobby.

"What a funny world this is!" remarked Tom, still amused. "Here is a man forever after rocks, rocks, and there goes a miner set upon becoming rich and discovering some imaginary mine."

He saw Jack waving to him from the veranda of the hotel.

"Listen, Tom," said his chum when they stood side by side, "I was thinking that it would be a splendid idea to send the Wondership to New York, and that from there we travel to Nestorville, *via* the air route."

"Great!" cried Tom, delighted. "But say, are we to take Masterson along?"

"Of course not," replied Jack. "He can go back to Boston on the train."

"Good for you!" declared Tom, slapping his chum on the back.

"But I haven't told you my main idea yet," said Jack, smiling,

"What is that?" asked the other wonderingly.

"Can't you guess?"

"No," Tom began to say, and then the roguish twinkle in Jack's eyes gave him a sudden inspiration. "You don't mean to use the Z.2.X. to send messages with while we fly nearer and nearer to our old home town?"

"That is exactly what I wish to do," said Jack quietly.

"Whoop! It's great!" cried Tom, throwing his hat in the air; and as he saw Dick coming toward them, he fairly pounced on the astonished reporter with the news.

"Flamjam flapcakes of Florida!" gasped Dick.

And so it was arranged. A few days later our party boarded a train for the East. Jack, Tom, Dick and Professor Jenks arrived at New York.

(They had left Zeb behind to attend to the work in the barren fields.)

The Wondership, as on the previous occasion, was quietly but quickly assembled, and made ready to take its homeward flight. They had chosen a spot on Manhattan island still very meagerly developed, and so were not at all troubled by curious onlookers. Jack, to whom his father had explained in detail the use of Z.2.X.—or Coloradite, as they had decided to call it—busied himself almost exclusively with the radio telephone apparatus. When all was ready, he sent his father the following telegram:

"Expect message, using Coloradite from New York."

The next morning they ascended. Round and round the Wondership circled, a golden speck against the blue sky. In a quarter of an hour the great metropolis seemed nothing but a giant beehive, with millions of busy workers ever hurrying in hundreds of different directions. The cars and automobiles were only like giant bees, moving somewhat swifter than those on what looked like fine threads of cotton or wool.

"What a small place New York is after all," observed the professor.

"It is larger than Boston," said Tom slyly,

"Perhaps," admitted the man of science haughtily, "but not as learned or stately—no city can take its culture away from Boston."

Jack smiled, and in order to change the conversation, asked Tom, "How high now?"

"About fifteen hundred feet," guessed Tom.

"Wrong," said Jack, glancing at the barograph on the dashboard in front of him. "We have reached two thousand eight hundred feet."

"I must be asleep," said Tom, frowning. "Shall I connect the alternator?"

Jack nodded and prepared to send greetings to his father, hundreds of miles away. They were out in the country now. As the Wondership glided through the air, the professor, in viewing the villages, farms, green pastures, and stretches of woodland, regretfully shook his head as the thought occurred to him that he was missing many a precious stone. He looked over to Jack with the idea of suggesting a descent, but he saw the boy inventor patiently adjusting the tuning knob, and waited, realizing how anxious Jack was to test the Coloradite.

The little professor, extremely interested, saw Jack place his lips to the receiver, and for the second time in his life, send out the distinct call:

"Hullo, High Towers!"

Many minutes passed without an answer. Jack's face became grave. Was part of the machinery not properly adjusted? He went over the instrument very carefully. In so far as he could see, everything was just as it should be. Then a thought came that made him dizzy—was it possible that the Coloradite was not suited for the work, that Mr. Chadwick had been misinformed?

"What's up?" inquired Tom, glancing up from his engines.

"By the ghost of Guzzlewits!" gasped Dick. "Don't say it won't work, Jack!"

The professor, ordinarily cool and very calculating, was strangely stirred. He watched the young inventor's face. Did it mean failure?

"I don't know," said Jack at last with forced calmness. "I will try again."

Once more Jack, oppressed by a vague fear, sent out the words:

"Hullo, High Towers!"

The reply came with startling swiftness, relieving the party from the mental strain. In one voice—the professor included—they yelled,

"Hurrah!"

"Congratulations!" came Mr. Chadwick's voice in return.

"Why the delay?" asked Jack, smiling with

"A small lever snapped. It required a few minutes to repair it. How far from New York are you now?"

"About forty miles."

"Good! Try to land here before sunset."

"Why?" asked Jack.

"Nestorville has a little surprise for you!" replied Mr. Chadwick, and Jack heard him chuckle.

"Good for Mr. Chadwick!" cried Dick in glee, for Jack had so arranged the instrument that all of them in the Wondership could hear Mr. Chadwick's voice.

Then followed a long conversation between father and son. Mr. Chadwick had almost completely recovered his health, and was again working over new experiments. Dick insisted that he be permitted to tell the story of their adventures on the island of the Coloradite Treasure.

"You won't tell it right," he declared to Jack, and insisted so strenuously that the boy inventor had to let him speak to Mr. Chadwick.

Dick set his choicest language agoing, and his vivid description of Jack's part in every incident was embellished by the most flowery adjectives in his vocabulary. Jack had to listen, and grin.

By the time his long story was done, Nestorville was sighted. As soon as the people saw the Wondership, pandemonium broke loose. Not only Nestorville, but officials and crowds from the neighboring towns had poured in, and the reception the boys and the professor received lingered with them for many, many years.

Later, as time went on, Mr. Chadwick's fortune was completely rehabilitated. Professor Jenks no longer was so eager to search for rocks, and while doing so get into all sorts of difficulties. He lived more at home, becoming at last, as his spinster sister declared, "a man with the proper spirit to make an ideal husband." Of course, the professor had received a very substantial sum of money from the boys.

Jack and Tom soon found themselves wealthy, and often in fancy trace the days back to that afternoon when they found the sturdy miner lying on the roadside, having been knocked unconscious by Masterson's careless driving of his automobile.

Zeb, continued to take charge of the work on Rattlesnake Island, to which the boys never returned. For a long time the supply from the black barren appeared to be inexhaustible. Suddenly, however, it ceased, and no more was dug. But what had been mined had been more than sufficient to make all prosperous.

Dick, with his share of the proceeds, which the boys insisted that he accept, bought the *Nestorville Bugle*. From the very start, he made it a live, progressive paper. Sometimes, when the now busy editor had a spare hour, he invariably visited his two friends, and the three—sometimes, too, the little professor joined them unexpectedly—recounted old-time stories.

But the boys were not made lazy by wealth and fame. To this very day, Jack and Tom, with Mr. Chadwick's aid, are devising many inventions calculated to benefit mankind. Possibly, at some future time, we shall hear something more about these, but for the present let us take our leave and say good-by.

Choose from Thousands of 1stWorldLibrary Classics By

A. M. Barnard	Booth Tarkington	Edward Everett Hale
Ada Leverson	Boyd Cable	Edward J. O'Biren
Adolphus William Ward	Bram Stoker	Edward S. Ellis
Aesop	C. Collodi	Edwin L. Arnold
Agatha Christie	C. E. Orr	Eleanor Atkins
Alexander Aaronsohn	C. M. Ingleby	Eleanor Hallowell Abbott
Alexander Kielland	Carolyn Wells	Eliot Gregory
Alexandre Dumas	Catherine Parr Traill	Elizabeth Gaskell
Alfred Gatty	Charles A. Eastman	Elizabeth McCracken
Alfred Ollivant	Charles Amory Beach	Elizabeth Von Arnim
Alice Duer Miller	Charles Dickens	Ellem Key
Alice Turner Curtis	Charles Dudley Warner	Emerson Hough
Alice Dunbar	Charles Farrar Browne	Emilie F. Carlen
Allen Chapman	Charles Ives	Emily Bronte
Alleyne Ireland	Charles Kingsley	Emily Dickinson
Ambrose Bierce	Charles Klein	Enid Bagnold
Amelia E. Barr	Charles Hanson Towne	Enilor Macartney Lane
Amory H. Bradford	Charles Lathrop Pack	Erasmus W. Jones
Andrew Lang	Charles Romyn Dake	Ernie Howard Pie
Andrew McFarland Davis	Charles Whibley	Ethel May Dell
Andy Adams	Charles Willing Beale	Ethel Turner
Angela Brazil	Charlotte M. Braeme	Ethel Watts Mumford
Anna Alice Chapin	Charlotte M. Yonge	Eugene Sue
Anna Sewell	Charlotte Perkins Stetson	Eugenie Foa
Annie Besant	Clair W. Hayes	Eugene Wood
Annie Hamilton Donnell	Clarence Day Jr.	Eustace Hale Ball
Annie Payson Call	Clarence E. Mulford	Evelyn Everett-green
Annie Roe Carr	Clemence Housman	Everard Cotes
Annonaymous	Confucius	F. H. Cheley
Anton Chekhov	Coningsby Dawson	F. J. Cross
Archibald Lee Fletcher	Cornelis DeWitt Wilcox	F. Marion Crawford
Arnold Bennett	Cyril Burleigh	Fannie E. Newberry
Arthur C. Benson	D. H. Lawrence	Federick Austin Ogg
Arthur Conan Doyle	Daniel Defoe	Ferdinand Ossendowski
Arthur M. Winfield	David Garnett	Fergus Hume
Arthur Ransome	Dinah Craik	Florence A. Kilpatrick
Arthur Schnitzler	Don Carlos Janes	Fremont B. Deering
Arthur Train	Donald Keyhoe	Francis Bacon
Atticus	Dorothy Kilner	Francis Darwin
B.H. Baden-Powell	Dougan Clark	Frances Hodgson Burnett
B. M. Bower	Douglas Fairbanks	Frances Parkinson Keyes
B. C. Chatterjee	E. Nesbit	Frank Gee Patchin
Baroness Emmuska Orczy	E. P. Roe	Frank Harris
Baroness Orczy	E. Phillips Oppenheim	Frank Jewett Mather
Basil King	E. S. Brooks	Frank L. Packard
Bayard Taylor	Earl Barnes	Frank V. Webster
Ben Macomber	Edgar Rice Burroughs	Frederic Stewart Isham
Bertha Muzzy Bower	Edith Van Dyne	Frederick Trevor Hill
Bjornstjerne Bjornson	Edith Wharton	Frederick Winslow Taylor

Friedrich Kerst
Friedrich Nietzsche
Fyodor Dostoyevsky
G.A. Henty
G.K. Chesterton
Gabrielle E. Jackson
Garrett P. Serviss
Gaston Leroux
George A. Warren
George Ade
Geroge Bernard Shaw
George Cary Eggleston
George Durston
George Ebers
George Eliot
George Gissing
George MacDonald
George Meredith
George Orwell
George Sylvester Viereck
George Tucker
George W. Cable
George Wharton James
Gertrude Atherton
Gordon Casserly
Grace E. King
Grace Gallatin
Grace Greenwood
Grant Allen
Guillermo A. Sherwell
Gulielma Zollinger
Gustav Flaubert
H. A. Cody
H. B. Irving
H.C. Bailey
H. G. Wells
H. H. Munro
H. Irving Hancock
H. R. Naylor
H. Rider Haggard
H. W. C. Davis
Haldeman Julius
Hall Caine
Hamilton Wright Mabie
Hans Christian Andersen
Harold Avery
Harold McGrath
Harriet Beecher Stowe
Harry Castlemon
Harry Coghill
Harry Houidini

Hayden Carruth
Helent Hunt Jackson
Helen Nicolay
Hendrik Conscience
Hendy David Thoreau
Henri Barbusse
Henrik Ibsen
Henry Adams
Henry Ford
Henry Frost
Henry James
Henry Jones Ford
Henry Seton Merriman
Henry W Longfellow
Herbert A. Giles
Herbert Carter
Herbert N. Casson
Herman Hesse
Hildegard G. Frey
Homer
Honore De Balzac
Horace B. Day
Horace Walpole
Horatio Alger Jr.
Howard Pyle
Howard R. Garis
Hugh Lofting
Hugh Walpole
Humphry Ward
Ian Maclaren
Inez Haynes Gillmore
Irving Bacheller
Isabel Cecilia Williams
Isabel Hornibrook
Israel Abrahams
Ivan Turgenev
J.G.Austin
J. Henri Fabre
J. M. Barrie
J. M. Walsh
J. Macdonald Oxley
J. R. Miller
J. S. Fletcher
J. S. Knowles
J. Storer Clouston
J. W. Duffield
Jack London
Jacob Abbott
James Allen
James Andrews
James Baldwin

James Branch Cabell
James DeMille
James Joyce
James Lane Allen
James Lane Allen
James Oliver Curwood
James Oppenheim
James Otis
James R. Driscoll
Jane Abbott
Jane Austen
Jane L. Stewart
Janet Aldridge
Jens Peter Jacobsen
Jerome K. Jerome
Jessie Graham Flower
John Buchan
John Burroughs
John Cournos
John F. Kennedy
John Gay
John Glasworthy
John Habberton
John Joy Bell
John Kendrick Bangs
John Milton
John Philip Sousa
John Taintor Foote
Jonas Lauritz Idemil Lie
Jonathan Swift
Joseph A. Altsheler
Joseph Carey
Joseph Conrad
Joseph E. Badger Jr
Joseph Hergesheimer
Joseph Jacobs
Jules Vernes
Julian Hawthrone
Julie A Lippmann
Justin Huntly McCarthy
Kakuzo Okakura
Karle Wilson Baker
Kate Chopin
Kenneth Grahame
Kenneth McGaffey
Kate Langley Bosher
Kate Langley Bosher
Katherine Cecil Thurston
Katherine Stokes
L. A. Abbot
L. T. Meade

L. Frank Baum
Latta Griswold
Laura Dent Crane
Laura Lee Hope
Laurence Housman
Lawrence Beasley
Leo Tolstoy
Leonid Andreyev
Lewis Carroll
Lewis Sperry Chafer
Lilian Bell
Lloyd Osbourne
Louis Hughes
Louis Joseph Vance
Louis Tracy
Louisa May Alcott
Lucy Fitch Perkins
Lucy Maud Montgomery
Luther Benson
Lydia Miller Middleton
Lyndon Orr
M. Corvus
M. H. Adams
Margaret E. Sangster
Margret Howth
Margaret Vandercook
Margaret W. Hungerford
Margret Penrose
Maria Edgeworth
Maria Thompson Daviess
Mariano Azuela
Marion Polk Angellotti
Mark Overton
Mark Twain
Mary Austin
Mary Catherine Crowley
Mary Cole
Mary Hastings Bradley
Mary Roberts Rinehart
Mary Rowlandson
M. Wollstonecraft Shelley
Maud Lindsay
Max Beerbohm
Myra Kelly
Nathaniel Hawthrone
Nicolo Machiavelli
O. F. Walton
Oscar Wilde
Owen Johnson
P.G. Wodehouse
Paul and Mabel Thorne

Paul G. Tomlinson
Paul Severing
Percy Brebner
Percy Keese Fitzhugh
Peter B. Kyne
Plato
Quincy Allen
R. Derby Holmes
R. L. Stevenson
R. S. Ball
Rabindranath Tagore
Rahul Alvares
Ralph Bonehill
Ralph Henry Barbour
Ralph Victor
Ralph Waldo Emmerson
Rene Descartes
Ray Cummings
Rex Beach
Rex E. Beach
Richard Harding Davis
Richard Jefferies
Richard Le Gallienne
Robert Barr
Robert Frost
Robert Gordon Anderson
Robert L. Drake
Robert Lansing
Robert Lynd
Robert Michael Ballantyne
Robert W. Chambers
Rosa Nouchette Carey
Rudyard Kipling
Saint Augustine
Samuel B. Allison
Samuel Hopkins Adams
Sarah Bernhardt
Sarah C. Hallowell
Selma Lagerlof
Sherwood Anderson
Sigmund Freud
Standish O'Grady
Stanley Weyman
Stella Benson
Stella M. Francis
Stephen Crane
Stewart Edward White
Stijn Streuvels
Swami Abhedananda
Swami Parmananda
T. S. Ackland

T. S. Arthur
The Princess Der Ling
Thomas A. Janvier
Thomas A Kempis
Thomas Anderton
Thomas Bailey Aldrich
Thomas Bulfinch
Thomas De Quincey
Thomas Dixon
Thomas H. Huxley
Thomas Hardy
Thomas More
Thornton W. Burgess
U. S. Grant
Upton Sinclair
Valentine Williams
Various Authors
Vaughan Kester
Victor Appleton
Victor G. Durham
Victoria Cross
Virginia Woolf
Wadsworth Camp
Walter Camp
Walter Scott
Washington Irving
Wilbur Lawton
Wilkie Collins
Willa Cather
Willard F. Baker
William Dean Howells
William le Queux
W. Makepeace Thackeray
William W. Walter
William Shakespeare
Winston Churchill
Yei Theodora Ozaki
Yogi Ramacharaka
Young E. Allison
Zane Grey